INSIGHT

D0115192

EXPLORE

ANDALUCÍA
& THE COSTA DEL SOL

attention circ:
check for map

◉ Walking Eye App

YOUR FREE EBOOK AVAILABLE THROUGH THE WALKING EYE APP

Your guide now includes a free eBook to your chosen destination, for the same great price as before. Simply download the Walking Eye App from the App Store or Google Play to access your free eBook.

HOW THE WALKING EYE APP WORKS

Through the Walking Eye App, you can purchase a range of eBooks and destination content. However, when you buy this book, you can download the corresponding eBook for free. Just see below in the grey panel where to find your free content and then scan the QR code at the bottom of this page.

Destinations: Download essential destination content featuring recommended sights and attractions, restaurants, hotels and an A–Z of practical information, all available for purchase.

Ships: Interested in ship reviews? Find independent reviews of river and ocean ships in this section, all available for purchase.

eBooks: You can download your free accompanying digital version of this guide here. You will also find a whole range of other eBooks, all available for purchase.

Free access to travel-related blog articles about different destinations, updated on a daily basis.

HOW THE EBOOKS WORK

The eBooks are provided in EPUB file format. Please note that you will need an eBook reader installed on your device to open the file. Many devices come with this as standard, but you may still need to install one manually from Google Play.

The eBook content is identical to the content in the printed guide.

HOW TO DOWNLOAD THE WALKING EYE APP

1. Download the Walking Eye App from the App Store or Google Play.
2. Open the app and select the scanning function from the main menu.
3. Scan the QR code on this page – you will then be asked a security question to verify ownership of the book.
4. Once this has been verified, you will see your eBook in the purchased ebook section, where you will be able to download it.

Other destination apps and eBooks are available for purchase separately or are free with the purchase of the Insight Guide book.

CONTENTS

EXCITING CITIES

Seville is full of interesting things to see and do (routes 1 and 2), but don't miss Cádiz and Jerez (route 5), Málaga (route 9), Córdoba (route 12) and Granada (route 15).

RECOMMENDED ROUTES FOR...

FAMILIES

Have a thrilling day out with the kids exploring the vertiginous path through a gorge on the Caminito del Rey (route 10) or take Gibraltar's cable car to meet the famous Barbary apes (route 7).

MOORISH TREASURES

Discover the amazingly ornate monuments built by Spain's long-lost Muslim civilisation: the fortress-palace of the Alhambra in Granada (route 16) and the Mezquita (Mosque) in the middle of Córdoba (route 12).

PANORAMIC VIEWS

Admire Seville's rooftops from its two prodigious viewpoints (routes 1 and 2) or gaze out to Morocco from atop the Rock of Gibraltar (route 7).

PICTURESQUE PUEBLOS

Ronda and the White Towns (route 6) are exquisite, as are the villages of the Alpujarras (route 17). The neighbouring towns of Úbeda and Baeza (route 13) are triumphs of Renaissance architecture.

SURF, SAND AND SUNSHINE

Take your pick of Andalucía's coasts and beaches, from the developed to the deserted on the Costa de la Luz (route 5), the Costa del Sol (routes 8 and 9), the Costa Tropical (route 18) and the coast of Almería (route 19).

THE GREAT OUTDOORS

Explore Andalucía's extraordinarily varied landscapes and discover its wildlife in Doñana National Park (route 3), the Sierra de Cazorla (route 14) and the desert cape of Almería, the Cabo de Gata (route 19).

WINE LOVERS

This is the home of sherry, and touring bodegas (wineries) can be a great way to spend a holiday. You'll find the best of them in Jerez de la Frontera (route 5) and Montilla (route 11).

INTRODUCTION

An introduction to Andalucía's geography, customs and culture, plus illuminating background information on cuisine, history and what to do when you're there.

Málaga's Teatro Romano

EXPLORE ANDALUCÍA

Andalucía is best known for the sun, sand and sea offered by its playground coasts, but that's only the half of it. The region is also extraordinarily rich in scenery, wildlife, history, art and culture.

With its bullfights, white towns, fans, flamenco music, fiestas and Mediterranean beaches, Andalucía is, to many visitors, 'typical Spain'. But it would be a mistake to see it as just a composite of these ingredients. This is a region made up of diverse landscapes – wild, open spaces and some of the highest mountains in Europe – and crowned by the vibrant cities of Seville, Córdoba and Granada, with their glorious Moorish monuments. Andalucía lies at a geographical crossroads: it is the gateway between the Mediterranean and the Atlantic, and the crossing point between Africa and Europe. The strategic importance of its location has given rise to a long and turbulent history. Over the centuries, the region has incorporated influences from many different sources, leaving it with an unparalleled heritage for the modern visitor to explore.

GEOGRAPHY AND LAYOUT

Andalucía runs right across Spain from the Portuguese border and the Atlantic in the west to the eastern Mediterranean coast. It is separated from central Spain (to the north) by the mountains of the Sierra Morena; in the south, a mere 14.5km (9 miles) of water – the Strait of Gibraltar – lie between Andalucía's tip and Morocco.

Andalucía is the second largest (but most populous) of the 17 autonomous regions of Spain, covering more than 17 percent of the country. It is sub-divided into eight provinces which are, going from west to east and north to south: Huelva, Seville, Cordoba, Jaen, Cadiz, Malaga, Granada and Almería. The coast of Malaga province is universally known as the Costa del Sol, a 180km (112-mile)-long chain of marinas, golf clubs and white urbanisations.

The routes in this book follow the provinces in this order as far as possible. Most of the routes – but not all – can be negotiated by public transport if you have time to wait for connections. Better, however, is to hire a car. Most visitors use either Seville (see routes 1 or 2) or Malaga (see route 9) as a base. All the towns and city centres described in the routes can be toured on foot.

Pretty in pink at Doñana National Park

HISTORY

Human occupation in Andalucía dates back to prehistoric times, evidenced by the Unesco World Heritage dolmens at Antequera (see page 45), Copper-Age Los Millares, and Palaeolithic cave paintings – some 25,000 years old. From the second millennium BC until the 8th century AD the region saw a wave of civilisations come and go: Iberians, Tartessians Phoenicians, Greeks, Carthaginians, Romans and Visigoths. Then, in 711, the Iberian peninsula was invaded by an army from North Africa; this event was to leave an indelible mark on Andalucía. The Muslim rulers of Spain – known for simplicity as the Moors – created the extraordinary Mezquita (Mosque) in Córdoba (see page 76) and the palace of the Alhambra in Granada (see page 89), as well as the renowned White Towns (see page 53) and numerous bathhouses and fortresses. In 1492 the last Moorish outpost, Granada, fell to a Christian army, heralding a new era for Spain. Christopher Columbus's historic voyage across the Atlantic turned Seville into a flourishing city, enriched by the wealth of the New World.

The good times didn't last, however, and centuries of stagnation and neglect followed. Unlike the north of Spain, Andalucía did not develop industry to create employment. Poverty and lack of work forced large numbers of Andalucíans (Andaluces) to emigrate. The devastating effects of the Spanish Civil War (1936–9) only made things worse.

Then, in the 1960s, holidaymakers from northern Europe discovered the potential of the Costa del Sol, which had strings of magnificent beaches almost entirely undeveloped and unfrequented. Tourism was the making of Andalucía – although it also brought challenges with regard to environmental protection and water conservation. Only with the advent of democracy and devolved government, following the death of General Franco in 1975, was Andalucía able to attract investment for its infrastructure and to fully modernise.

CLIMATE

Andalucía's position at the southern edge of Europe gives it an excellent climate. Summers are hot, winters mild – and plentiful sunshine makes it possible to sit outside practically year-round. Swimming in the sea, at the region's sheltered beaches and coves, is warm enough from spring through autumn.

However, there are considerable variations due to the size of the region, its mountainous character and the fact that it is bordered by both the Atlantic and Mediterranean. Summers can be exceptionally hot in the interior, in the provinces of Seville and Córdoba. Almería, meanwhile, has an extremely arid, desert-like climate. Snow covers the Sierra Nevada from November to June. Not far away, the Costa Tropical is so-named because of a

Gitano woman

microclimate that allows tropical fruits to be grown. The Atlantic coast is known for its strong winds. In general, spring and early summer are the best times to visit Andalucía – to avoid the most oppressive heat, not to mention the crowds and high-season hotel rates, and to admire the countryside, at its best with wildflowers in bloom.

POPULATION

Andalucía is the most populous region in Spain with over 8.3 million inhabitants (almost 18 percent of the Spanish total). It has always been a place in movement: dispatching emigrants in search of work to northern Spain and Europe, and receiving immigrants in its turn. The immigrant population is from both north and sub-Saharan Africa and, in marked contrast, northern Europe – mainly wealthy immigrants lured by the agreeable climate and relaxed lifestyle.

The last few decades have witnessed a shift of people from the countryside to the cities, many chasing jobs and the allure of modern city life. The Andalucían population is, predictably, concentrated in the provincial capitals and along the Costa del Sol.

Gitanos

Andalucía's 300,000 gypsies (*gitanos*) comprise the region's largest ethnic minority, making up 3 percent of the population. Their level of integration varies enormously. Some gypsies proudly reject the values of *payo* (non-gypsy) culture and as a result are often marginalised, with high rates of illiteracy and other forms of social deprivation. Others, however, fit seamlessly into mainstream society. The first gypsies arrived in Spain in the 15th century, and for centuries were discriminated against and persecuted. Modern laws forbid all racial and ethnic discrimination. It is impossible to overestimate the impact the gypsies have had on the region, and sometimes – as seen in flamenco music and dance and all its derivatives – it is impossible to differentiate between gypsy and Andalucían culture.

LOCAL CUSTOMS

Every Spanish stereotype, cliché and hyperbole comes to roost in Andalucía and it is easy to be taken in by them. It is true that Andalucíans generally live at a slower pace than in the frenetic cities of northern Europe, that they take pleasure in everything and that they get less stressed by punctuality. Patience is often required; everything gets done at its appropriate pace.

It is essential that you, as a visitor, get into the rhythm of long life. The morning is long. Lunch is eaten from 2pm and this is followed by a period of rest when some people sleep a siesta. This is not a sign of laziness but a shrewd way to pass the heat of the day when it isn't

Seville's cathedral   *Brotherhood of El Beso de Judas procession*

possible to do anything outside. Many monuments and museums close for a long midday break from 1 to 5pm. This needs to be incorporated into your touring plans.

Dinner is similarly 'late', beginning at 9pm. Andalucíans only go out for the night after 10 or 11pm. They stay out late and take their children with them. Miraculously, whatever they have been up to the night before, everyone gets up early for work the next morning.

Although few people attend church for more than weddings and funerals, Spanish society is nominally Catholic and you should show respect when visiting churches, cathedrals and monasteries, or attending traditional religious fiestas.

Most Andalucíans are highly sociable, usually willing to strike up a conversation with an interested visitor who speaks only a few words of Spanish. English is spoken on the coasts and in the cities, but elsewhere it will have to be you who makes the effort.

DON'T LEAVE ANDALUCÍA WITHOUT...

Exploring the Alhambra. One of the world's greatest monuments, the exquisite Moorish fortress-palace above Granada was designed to be a piece of paradise on earth. See page 89.

Wandering around the Mosque of Córdoba. The ancient Mezquita is a marvel of sacred architecture, a graceful forest of slender pillars and elaborate arches. See page 76.

Climbing La Giralda in Seville. The bell tower of the cathedral is easily ascended (by ramp) for a magnificent view over the rooftops of Andalucía's capital. See page 31.

Sampling fino. Jerez de la Frontera is famous for its sherry wines. The favourite variety in Andalucía is a strong, dry white wine that makes a perfect aperitif on a hot summer's day. See page 47.

Crossing the bridge between the two parts of Ronda. The white town of Ronda is dramatically sited on the lip of a cliff and divided by a gaping ravine. See page 55.

Ordering a round of tapas. In Andalucía, you always eat a little something with your drink. In Granada, the tapas are complimentary. Everywhere else they are inexpensive and always tasty. See page 18.

Attending a fiesta. There is always a traditional festival going on somewhere, especially at Easter and during the summer months, providing free street entertainment. See page 125.

Walking the Caminito del Rey. Navigating this dizzying footpath clinging to the side of a gorge makes a memorable day out. See page 67.

Seeing a flamenco show. Seville, Jerez de la Frontera and Sacromonte in Granada are good places to catch a performance of the moving music and dance of Andalucía. See page 22.

POLITICS AND ECONOMICS

The autonomous region of Andalucía is ruled by the Junta de Andalucía (Government of Andalucía), complete with its own parliament and president, based in Seville. It controls a budget of more than 30,000 billion euros and employs around 250,000 people directly, most of them in education or healthcare. Since the transition to democracy after Franco's death, Andalucía has been governed by the Socialist PSOE party.

Andalucía is one of the least prosperous Spanish regions, low on natural resources and the recipient of much grant aid from Madrid and the EU. Spain, as a whole, is doing well, its economy having picked up since the economic crisis of 2008, but not everyone has gained. Andalucía has a higher level of poverty than any other Spanish region and one of the highest levels of unemployment of all EU regions. You are unlikely to notice this in tourist areas. Tourism is one of the mainstays of the economy, although there is still an important level of agricultural production.

LANDSCAPE AND WILDLIFE

With so much going on, it's easy to forget the natural backdrop. One of the great attractions of Andalucía is the variety of its landscapes, which range from forests in Cazorla (see page 83) to deserts in Almería (see page 100), by way of the neat ranks of olive trees that cover so much of the provinces of Jaén and Córdoba. The areas of wine production are – naturally – veiled in vines.

A total of 17 percent of the region is afforded official protection as natural wilderness, more than triple the national average. In all, there are more than 80 different locations classified as nature park (*parquet natural*), nature reserve (*reserve natural*) or nature enclave (*paraje natural*) – from small, inaccessible lagoons that are crucial to migrating birds, to vast forested tracts, such as the Cazorla nature park (see page 83). The jewel in the crown of wild Andalucía is the Doñana National Park (see page 39), spreading 542 sq km (209 sq miles) at the mouth of the Guadalquivir river. Home of the endangered Iberian lynx, this important wetland site offers some stunning scenery and experiences to nature lovers.

Mostly what you'll notice is the mountainous nature of Andalucía. The highest mountain in mainland Spain, Mulhacén (3,478 metres/11,411ft), is in the Sierra Nevada south of Granada. Pick the right day in winter and it is possible to go skiing in the morning and swimming on the Costa Tropical (see page 98) in the afternoon.

What sums up the whole of this region and its people? Not much, except that when you think you know it well there's certain to be a surprise waiting for you around the corner.

Parque Natural de las Sierras de Cazorla, Segura y Las Villas

TOP TIPS FOR VISITING ANDALUCÍA

Late habits. Everything starts late in Andalucía. Lunch is not usually until 2pm and dinner not until at least 9 or 10pm. That's when a night out begins – live-music venues and clubs do not get going until 2am. It is best to get into the rhythm of local life rather than sticking to your habitual hours. Pace yourself, be patient and take advantage of the long morning to do things at a leisurely pace. Expect many shops and most monuments to be closed for two or three hours over lunchtime.

Sun and heat. The sun in southern Spain can be fiercer than you think. Pack a hat, use sun cream and stay in the shade as much as possible while you acclimatise. Always carry water with you to prevent dehydration. Having a siesta is a good idea: life resumes when the cool descends in the evening and you need to recover your energy for the night ahead.

Ask for what you need. Andalucíans are generally obliging and even stern-looking officials may be willing to make an exception for you if you ask in a polite way. But they may not be able to guess what you want or whether you need help. Always start by saying '*buenos días*' or '*hola*' before you say anything else, then explain the situation as best you can. You may have to be patient while waiting for someone to comply with a request: things don't move at the same frenetic pace in Andalucía as they often do in northern Europe.

Fiestas. When there's a fiesta on, don't expect to do sightseeing as usual. Traffic and crowds increase and hotels get booked up. It's best to go with the flow and enjoy the events rather than visiting the museums and monuments.

Distances, hills and curves. Much of Andalucía is mountainous. Distances between places can be more than you expect, and away from the motorways you should be prepared for roads that mostly wind and climb over passes to get from one place to the next.

Eat while you drink. Tapas exist for a reason – to accompany (mainly) alcoholic drinks. Do as the locals do, and order some food. Without it, the heat can send the alcohol straight to your head and you may pay for it later.

Respect the local culture. A little interest in how people live and think will open doors for you. Ask polite, intelligent questions and you may well get invited on an impromptu tour, say, of a winery. This goes for the tricky subject of bullfighting, too. While some Andalucíans are heartily opposed to it, for many it is an integral part of their culture. Inform yourself about it and try to see it from their point of view rather than rejecting it out of hand.

Menú del día. Every restaurant serves a fixed-price lunchtime menu, which is an economical way to eat. You usually get three hearty courses with bread and perhaps a carafe of wine for a low price (€10–20).

Sardines take the heat

FOOD AND DRINK

Great food and drink are not just an extra to a holiday in Andalucía; they are one of the highlights. The region excels in fish and seafood, complemented by a rich array of fresh vegetables.

Andalucía is blessed with an abundance of good things to eat from both land and sea. Top restaurants may aim to serve haute cuisine, but for authentic food you can't do better than eat where the locals eat and order what they do. There are plenty of restaurants that don't look anything special from the outside but which serve hearty, healthy homemade dishes based on excellent raw ingredients, washed down with a glass or two of the local wine. Whether or not there is a menu in the bar or restaurant where you find yourself, don't be afraid to tell a waiter exactly what you want: usually he or she, and the rest of the staff, will be happy to oblige.

EATING HOURS

First-time visitors to Spain are often surprised by the late eating hours: the Spanish rarely sit down to lunch (*almuerzo*), the main meal of the day, before 2pm and dinner (*cena*) starts around 9 or 10pm. In resorts you will be able to eat much earlier than this and many restaurants stay open throughout the day. Any bar will always fill a hungry gap: it will usually make you what you want to order.

BREAKFAST

Spaniards normally eat a light breakfast and often have a more substantial snack midmorning. In Andalucía it is common to order toast spread with tomato puree, drizzled with olive oil and sprinkled with salt to taste. If you prefer jam and butter, be sure to specify. Resort hotels often offer a buffet breakfast and in internationally orientated bars and restaurants a full English breakfast isn't hard to find.

SOUPS

Andalucía's most famous speciality is the cold soup known as *gazpacho*. There are literally dozens of ways to make it, but the version you are likely to find on menus is a chilled blend of cucumber, tomato and crushed garlic, occasionally accompanied by freshly diced green pepper, tomato, cucumber, chopped hard-boiled egg and fried croutons on the side.

Fresh gazpacho   *Seafood paella*

Ajo blanco (white garlic soup) is a variation on the more common gazpacho theme. Ground almonds and garlic form the base of this summer refresher, served ice-cold with a garnish of almonds and grapes.

For something hot, try a mixed fish (*sopa de pescado*) or shellfish soup (*sopa de mariscos*) or a catchall *sopa marinera* based on the day's catch and seasoned with tomato, onion, garlic and a dash of white wine or brandy.

PAELLA

Spain's most famous dish, which the Spaniards usually eat at lunchtime, originated in Valencia but is widely served in Andalucían restaurants as either a first or second course. The main ingredient of paella is saffron-flavoured rice, cooked with a variety of vegetables and either chicken or seafood (prawns, mussels and other shellfish).

SEAFOOD

The seafood you are served in the waterfront restaurants was probably landed on the beach that very morning by the fishermen whose boats lie hauled up on the sand. For a straightforward meal order sardines skewered on a wooden spike and grilled over a charcoal fire on the beach. This simple but tasty dish is irresistible and extremely good value. Squid may be an interesting option, either cooked in its own ink (*calamares en su tinta*), a spicy dish, or simply dipped in batter and fried, and served with a twist of lemon. *Gambas, langostinos* and *cigalas* are large juicy prawns – choose your own from the display and have them grilled while you select your wine.

Langosta (lobster) is excellent served hot with butter or cold with mayonnaise. *Boquerones* (fresh anchovies) and *chanquetes* (whitebait) are tossed in flour and deep-fried whole. *Boquerones* may also be prepared ceviche-style, marinated raw in oil and lemon with garlic and parsley. *Merluza*, or hake, may be served fried, boiled or mushroom-stuffed, perhaps with tomatoes and potatoes. *Besugo* (sea bream) is a high-quality fish, which is brushed with olive oil and simply grilled.

Other common items on the menu may include *pez espada* (swordfish), *mero* (sea bass), *bonito* (tuna) and *rape* (monkfish).

Note that fish is sometimes priced on the menu by weight, so what appears to be an inexpensive dish may prove very costly.

DESSERT

Dessert in Andalucía usually means a choice between two things: an egg and caramel custard known as *flan* (but always ask if it is homemade) or fresh fruit in season which may include *uvas* (grapes), *higos* (figs), *melón* (melon), *naranjas* (oranges), *meloco-*

tones (peaches), *chirimoyas* (custard apples), *fresas* (strawberries) or *cerezas* (cherries).

VEGETARIANS

It's not easy for vegetarians to eat out in Spain, although times are changing. It is not uncommon for restaurants to mark dishes on the menu as suitable for vegetarians or for other dietary requirements, and although many of Andalucía's signature dishes contain meat or fish, restaurant staff will generally do what they can for you. They may leave out an ingredient or bump up a meat-free starter or side dish into a main course if requested, or provide something that is not on the menu – even if it is only a plain omelette (*tortilla francesa*). On the plus side, there are some excellent vegetable dishes and soups and salads that do not depend on meat. All that said, however, older people in rural areas may regard meat as a sign of prosperity and good times, so don't make too much of a moral issue out of it. Veganism may be difficult to cater for. Some restaurants will serve gluten-free meals if asked.

TAPAS

People in Andalucía do not like to drink without eating a little something, hence the existence of tapas. *Tapa* means a lid. Tapas are believed to have originated in Andalucía during the 19th century; when someone ordered a wine, a slice of ham or sausage was served on a saucer and placed atop the glass as a 'lid' to keep the flies out.

Often tapas are displayed on the bar and you can point to what you want, but sometimes they are made to order.

In Granada province you get a tapa free shortly after your drink has arrived – don't order any more food until you have had the tapa. Everywhere else you pay for your tapas; be aware that a succession of them can soon add up.

Tapas may be hot or cold. The simplest tapas consist of a few olives, nuts or crisps – enough to form an appetiser before you move on to a meal. Anywhere along the coast you will probably be served prawns or fried fish.

If you can't see any tapas in sight and you want to eat something quick and uncomplicated, ask for Russian salad, ham or *tortilla de patata* – three standards that all bars have on hand.

If you want a larger amount of any tapa, request a *ración*. Your waiter may ask you to confirm that this is what you want and if you are not sure, you can play safe and order a *media* (half) *ración* to begin with. Note that tapas are ordered and priced individually so a meal entirely of tapas can easily end up costing more than a set restaurant menu.

Andalucía's liquid gold is one of Spain's most famous exports

MENÚ DEL DÍA

Every restaurant in Spain offers a three-course *menú del día* on weekday lunchtimes, which is often extremely good value. A pitcher of house wine and coffee may or may not be included. In the simplest restaurants there will be no written menu: your waiter will reel off the choices and you'll have to decide on the spot. A *menú de degustacion* is something entirely different: a sampler menu of the best the restaurant has to offer, usually at a price.

DRINKS

Wine
An aristocrat among wines, *Jerez* (sherry) is produced from grapes grown in the chalky vineyards around Jerez de la Frontera. It is aged in casks by blending the young wine with a transfusion of mature sherry, a method known as *solera*. *Fino*, the driest of the sherries, is a light, golden aperitif that should be served chilled. A type of *fino* called *manzanilla* is slightly richer; Sanlúcar de Barrameda *manzanilla* is especially good. *Amontillado*, usually medium dry, is a deeper gold in colour, and is heavier than a true *fino*. *Amoroso* is medium sweet, with an amber colour, and *oloroso* is still more full-bodied. Cream sherries are not popular in Spain.

Sherry-type wines are also made in the Montilla-Moriles region near Córdoba. Andalucía produces several other semisweet to sweet wines, most notably the mahogany-coloured wine of Málaga, called *Málaga dulce* (rather like port).

Table wines are also produced here, such as the whites from the Condado de Huelva region and reds from some of the highest vineyards in Europe, located on the slopes of the Contraviesa in Granada. Many restaurants will sell their own house wine, which may be a young wine that is produced locally. Wines from other regions of Spain are widely available, notably rich reds from Rioja and sparkling wines (cava) from Catalunya.

Beer
Beer in Spain (*cerveza*) always means chilled lager. There are many Andalucían brands available by the bottle or on draft (*presion*). It is now possible to order a stronger, more malty beer: ask for *cerveza tostada*. In the coastal resorts – and certainly in Gibraltar – you can order a pint of British beer.

Coffee
Coffee is a treat in Spain. There are various ways to order it: *café solo* is an expresso and *café con leche* is a coffee with hot, steamy milk. *Café cortado* is a black coffee with just a splash of milk. If you want a longer, weaker coffee, ask for an *Americano*. Every barista in Andalucía is used to dealing with a variety of preferences for drinks: just say clearly what you want.

Flamenco dresses and paintings for sale

SHOPPING

In Andalucía, shopping is a sociable act. You're certain to get interacting with the locals while you hunt for that special something to take home as a souvenir or present.

Shopping can be one of the great pleasures of a holiday in Andalucía, whether you dedicate time to it or just stop and browse according to your fancy en route. Whatever you do, don't leave it to the last minute at the airport, where you will be charged high prices for a reduced selection of goods.

WHERE TO SHOP

Andalucía has an enormous variety of places to shop, ranging from swanking chain boutiques to side-of-the-road pop-up stalls selling cut-price crafts. As a general rule, the best shopping is wherever tourists don't congregate: in beach resorts you'll probably pay more for less choice and inferior quality.

Shopping centres and hypermarkets are the same the world over, but their content is tailored to a local clientele and you can find unusual items if you look for them. Smaller shops are not necessarily less well stocked or more expensive, and if you dare to go in the chances are you will be rewarded with an interesting conversation.

Something of a good compromise is a department store. El Corte Inglés department store has branches in all the major cities of Andalucía. They stock a little of everything and the quality is generally good.

For more sophisticated shopping you have to go where the beautiful people go. Marbella, especially Puerto Banús, has dozens of high-end boutiques offering a stunning selection of merchandise, at equally stunning prices.

Markets

Every large town has a weekly open-air market held on a specific day of the week. This is likely to be a mix of food, household goods and cut-price clothing. Big cities have at least one permanent covered market and street markets (*mercadillos*) in the suburbs. You may also see flea markets and car-boot sales – probably called *rastro* or *rastrillo* – advertised locally.

WHAT TO BUY

Typical souvenirs

Many visitors to Andalucía are happy with *botas* (wineskins), castanets, Span-

Tourist stalls in the Albaicín, Granada

ish dolls, flamenco dresses and bull-fighting posters. If you are going to buy such souvenirs, at least ensure they are made locally – but it's better to look for an authentic, specialised shop rather than buy them from a general store on the beach.

One typical Andalucían accessory needs special mention. A fan is elegant, portable and practical – you'll appreciate it on a hot summer's night without a breeze. Shop carefully, however. Fans range from cheap plastic imports to exquisitely made craft items with a price to match. The cheap variety does the job just as well, but a well-made fan can last you a lifetime.

Crafts

By far the best souvenirs are local handmade products, preferably purchased directly from the people who make them. As you travel around you will see a number of craft shops and workshops, often creating employment in rural areas. Crafts, of course, take time and skill to make and if the price seems high, reflect for a moment on what you are buying. It makes sense to buy one good piece that you love, even if it is a little dear, than several mass-produced items you will soon tire of.

Local crafts from Andalucía include ceramics (Purullena near Guadix), blankets and rugs (Grazalema and the Alpujarras), baskets and wickerwork,

marquetry, silver jewellery and guitars (notably from Granada).

Food and drink

You will probably eat and drink well in Andalucía and some items, properly packed and protected, can be taken home to enjoy later when you need to remember the sunshine and good life.

Wine

Andalucía produces some excellent wines. Fortified wines are produced in Jerez de la Frontera and Montilla, near Cordoba. Sweet wines are made in the Malaga region. You can buy all these direct from producers or in supermarkets.

Ham

Jamón serrano, the variety of ham which is cured in the dry air of the mountains in Trevelez in the Alpujarras and in the Sierra de Aracena in Huelva, is considered a gourmet treat. It is available in sealed packets in supermarkets.

Olives and olive oil

Olives are the staple crop in the provinces of Jaén and Córdoba where olive oil is treated with a reverence akin to that afforded to wines. Fish, croquettes, pork and potatoes are all fried in olive oil. A small bottle of extra virgin olive oil will provide a little taste of Andalucía to take home with you.

ENTERTAINMENT

There's always something going on in Andalucía, especially along the coasts and in the cities. It ranges from free entertainment in the streets provided by traditional fiestas to world-class classical and rock concerts and international arts festivals.

In such a sociable outdoors region, going out for the night is an integral part of life. Andalucía offers a wide choice of entertainment from low- to highbrow. A night out begins later than in northern Europe and goes on later, especially in summer when daytime temperatures are too hot to do anything except stay indoors.

plays – but almost always in Spanish. In smaller towns, particularly seaside resorts, you often see one-off performances, sometimes for children. The cities all have cinemas, and while most films are dubbed, you can sometimes find one shown in the original language with subtitles.

FINDING OUT WHAT'S ON

Local tourist information offices are the best places to find out about concerts, theatre, cinema, exhibitions and other events taking place nearby during your stay. There are also likely to be posters up outside the town hall (*ayuntamiento*). To find out what's coming up visit the Guía del Ocio website (www.guiadelocio.com), which has a pull-down menu for each major city. Another source of information on the Costa del Sol is one of the free English-language newspapers, such as SUR in English – available in supermarkets and elsewhere.

THEATRE AND FILM

All the major cities have renowned theatres putting on a full programme of

MUSIC AND DANCE

Whatever your taste in music, you are likely to find it catered for. There is an emphasis on Spanish music, particularly flamenco, but you can also hear blues and jazz in the unlikeliest places if you ask around.

Flamenco

Flamenco is the traditional music of Andalucía, especially of the gypsy community. It is unmistakeable when you hear it.

The emotion-filled voice of a flamenco singer expressing torment and sadness is often only accompanied by rhythmic clapping, but to this is usually added the brisk strumming of a guitar. Sometimes the guitarist and hand-clappers provide the rhythm for a dancer

Lope de Vega Theatre, Seville

– usually, but not always, female and wearing a tightly fitting colourful dress.

Flamenco is an ancient art form, combining elements of Visigothic, Moorish and gypsy music, song and dance. There are two distinct types: the *cante jondo* (deep song), an intense outpouring of emotion; and the animated *cante chico* (light song). There are also different varieties of flamenco dance, including the *tango, fandango, farruca* and *zambra*, performed to the staccato rhythms and counter-rhythms of the castanets, hand clapping (*palmadas*) and finger snapping (*pitos*), as well as furious heel-drumming (*zapateado*).

Flamenco is usually associated with the provinces of Seville and Cádiz, but there are venues (*tablaos*) in all major Andalucían cities. Prices are generally not cheap, but often a drink or dinner is included. There is no need to understand Spanish to enjoy the spectacle – you simply have to feel the music.

Some flamenco is tailored to the tastes of tourists. A purist would say that if tourists are watching it, it can't be the real thing – but this is simplistic. Flamenco is in constant evolution. It has hybridised in a thousand equally valid ways and it is, when reduced to its essentials, a form of entertainment.

One good place to find out more is the Museo de Flamenco in Seville (Calle Manuel Rojas Marcos 3 tel 954 340 311; www.museoflamenco.com).

Another option is to attend a flamenco festival. The most important takes place in Seville in August every two years (even years; www.labienal. com). In the intervening years, the festival is held in Málaga (www.malagaen flamenco.com). Other festivals take place in Jerez de la Frontera (April) and Ronda and Granada (August).

BULLFIGHTING

Is bullfighting a legitimate form of entertainment? To some people it is that and more: it is a tradition; an art; and an indispensable part of Spanish culture. Nowhere in Spain, with the possible exception of Madrid, is bullfighting as exalted as in Andalucía. Indeed, bullfighting has been said to be right at the heart of the Andalucían character in the way it epitomises courage, nobility and grace in the face of mortal challenge. To be a *figura de torero* earns huge respect and status.

Bullfighting is hugely controversial, internationally and at home. There is a thriving animal-rights movement in Spain that would like to see the *corrida* banned for its cruelty and torment. But, like it or loathe it, the 'sport' is an ingrained part of Spanish culture, and its popularity is – somewhat surprisingly – on the rise. As a tourist, you have the chance to avoid it completely or to find out what the fuss is all about and make up your own mind. Bullfighting is sometimes televised but for an authentic experience you need to attend one of the 70 bullrings operating in Andalucía. Ronda's is one of the oldest in Spain.

Snorkelling near Tarifa

ACTIVITIES

Travelling around the sights or lazing on a beach can be a great way to spend a holiday, but sometimes you need to do more. Andalucía has the perfect ingredients for getting active: an outdoors climate and swathes of lovely coast and countryside.

Andalucía offers an extraordinary range of things to do, and sports facilities are there in abundance to help work off the effects of too much paella. Water sports are an obvious attraction and the Costa del Sol is famed for its golf courses, but it doesn't stop there. The region's countryside – notably the Alpujarras, the Serranía de Ronda and the nature park of Cazorla – are great places for hiking or horse riding. Surprisingly, too, one of Spain's largest ski resorts is only an hour from the south coast.

BEACHES AND WATERSPORTS

The coasts of Andalucía are remarkably different; there is a beach to suit everyone. The Costa del Sol is mostly built up, but with 160km (100 miles) of coastline, there are still coves where you can escape the crowds. If you want to be sure of finding somewhere quiet and void of faceless touristic infrastructure, try the Atlantic beaches off the coast of Cadiz (see page 49), although the west coast tends to be very windy, or the beaches of Almería's eastern 'Desert' coast (see page 100). The Costa Tropical (the coast of Granada) is something of a happy medium.

For truly unfrequented beaches, you will probably have to ask the locals for directions and be prepared to walk some way from the car park.

All tourist resorts offer a range of water sports: windsurfing, canoeing and pedalos. Several have marinas where sailing boats both large and small are moored. For surfing proper you need to go to Tarifa (see page 51).

UNDERWATER

Snorkelling can be an engrossing activity, particularly along rocky sections of the Andalucían coastline – you'll see far more than off sandy beaches. If you want to take it further, opt for a scuba-diving lesson or, if you are experienced, enjoy a trip into the blue with a private company. A popular dive spot is off La Herradura on the Costa Tropical (see page 99). For more information, contact FAAS, the Federación Andaluza de Actividades Acuaticas, faas.com.es.

SKIING

For three to four months each winter, depending on regional weather patterns,

Marbella golf course · *Family fun on the Costa del Sol*

the Sierra Nevada northeast of Granada becomes Europe's most southerly ski resort. Around half an hour by bus from Granada, the resort has over 50 slopes, from nursery to black runs, skiboard runs and toboggan routes, as well as accommodation ranging from youth hostels to four-star hotels. The resort has online reservations and a phone line offering weather reports and reservations. Theoretically, it is possible to spend a day skiing and have dinner by the Mediterranean. For more information, see sierranevada.es.

GOLF

Andalucía has around 130 golf courses, almost half of them on the Costa del Sol. Many are of competition standard. Most courses are open to visitors in return for a day's green fees and clubs, caddies and carts are generally available for hire. Some hotels specifically cater for golfing holidays. To find a course, see the website of the Real Federacion Espanola de Golf, www.rfegolf.es.

HIKING

Southern Spain's landscape is extraordinarily varied and boasts some excellent walking country. Find the right patch of hillside strewn with wild flowers beneath high-altitude crags overflown by eagles and vultures, or a wooded valley alive with birdsong and the trickle of water, and there is no better place to be out of doors.

Spring and early summer are the best times to go walking in Andalucía, when the landscape is smothered in wild flowers but the days are not too hot. The Mediterranean vegetation burns dry in the heat of July and August, although these are good months to go walking at higher, normally snow-capped altitudes. Autumn and winter are good for exploring the countryside near the coasts when the access roads aren't clogged with tourist traffic.

Whenever and wherever you go walking, common-sense advice applies: stick to walks on marked paths within your ability; never walk alone; take the best map you can find; and make sure someone knows where you have gone and when you expect to be back. Wear proper walking shoes (boots are best), a hat and something warm if you are going to any altitude. Always carry plenty of drinking water.

ACTIVITIES FOR CHILDREN

A theme park will keep the kids happy. The biggest ones are Tivoli World (www.tivoli.es) on the Costa del Sol and Isla Mágica (www.islamagica.es) in Seville. A water park with its slides and pools will also be popular – there is one near each major city. In Gibraltar you can combine a cable car ride with seeing semi-wild monkeys. Other possibilities are a train or boat trip, birdwatching in Doñana National Park (see page 39) or a walk along the Caminito del Rey (see page 67).

Alcázar de los Reyes Cristianos garden, Córdoba

HISTORY: KEY DATES

Andalucía has seen a succession of civilisations and rulers come and go over its long history. Each has left behind a rich legacy of architecture, achievement, culture and legend that has been added to the region's melting pot.

EARLIEST TIMES

700,000 BC	Suggested date for the earliest human habitation in Andalucía.
1100 BC	Phoenician traders settle in Cádiz.
800–550 BC	The Tartessos civilisation thrives near Huelva and Cádiz.
218–201 BC	Romans occupy Iberia.
407–415	Germanic tribes occupy Spain; Visigothic kingdom established.

THE MOORS

711	Tariq ibn-Ziyad, a Berber commander, lands at Gibraltar and launches the Islamic conquest of the Iberian Peninsula.
720	Christians defeat Muslims at Covadonga in northernmost Spain, initiating the 'Reconquest' of Iberia, which is to take 772 years.
929	Caliphate of Córdoba founded.
1010–13	The Caliphate of Córdoba breaks up into petty kingdoms.
1147	Almohads invade Spain from North Africa.
1211	Christian armies defeat Moors at Las Navas de Tolosa.
1236	Córdoba conquered by Fernando III; Seville follows in 1248.
1340	Islamic forces are defeated at the battle of Río Salado, ending all efforts of invasion from northern Africa.
1348	Black Death sweeps through Spain.
1391	Widespread pogroms against Jews.
1474	Isabel becomes Queen of Castile.
1481	Inquisition instituted in Spain.

THE AGE OF EMPIRE

1492	Fernando and Isabel conquer Granada, last Moorish kingdom in Spain; Columbus discovers America.

Spanish coins during the Franco era

| 1519 | Magellan sets sail from Sanlúcar de Barrameda to circumnavigate the world. |
| 1587 | While the Armada prepares to invade England, Sir Francis Drake attacks Cádiz and sets fire to the Spanish fleet. |

18TH AND 19TH CENTURIES

1701–13	Spanish King Carlos II dies childless, sparking War of Spanish Succession; Treaty of Utrecht grants throne to the Bourbon pretender; Gibraltar is ceded to Great Britain.
1779–83	Great Siege of Gibraltar by Spanish and French.
1808	Napoleon replaces Spanish king with his brother, Joseph Bonaparte; Spaniards revolt against occupying French army.
1812	Spain's first constitution is drafted in Cádiz.
1885	Devastating earthquake kills hundreds and destroys thousands of homes in the provinces of Granada and Málaga.

20TH CENTURY TO THE PRESENT

1923	Primo de Rivera seizes control as dictator, with Alfonso XIII remaining as king.
1929	Ibero-American Exposition in Seville.
1931	Spain becomes a republic.
1936	Spanish army revolts, led by General Franco, and three-year Spanish Civil War begins.
1939	Spanish Civil War ends with Franco's victory.
1955	Spain joins the United Nations.
1969	Spain closes border with Gibraltar – it reopens 16 years later.
1975	Franco dies, and Spain becomes constitutional monarchy. First free elections are held in 1977.
1982	Andalucía becomes an autonomous region.
1986	Spain joins European Community.
2002	The euro replaces the peseta.
2008	Spain is badly affected by the global financial crisis.
2014	King Juan Carlos I abdicates and his son is crowned Felipe VI.
2016	Following a second general election in six months, the People's Party under Mariano Rajoy forms a minority government.
2018	Andalucía expected to receive a record 30 million tourists.

BEST ROUTES

Puerta de San Cristóbal

SEVILLE CITY CENTRE AND SANTA CRUZ

Andalucía's capital is one of the world's most beautiful cities, exuding a sensual and romantic atmosphere. This tour visits the city's priority sights: the cathedral and its iconic bell tower, the royal palace and the exquisitely pretty Santa Cruz quarter.

DISTANCE: 1.5 km (1 mile)
TIME: half a day or 1 day
START & END: Plaza del Triunfo
POINTS TO NOTE: Allow time for queuing to buy cathedral tickets: get there as early as you can. Reserve your ticket for the Alcázar in advance; you will be asked choose a half-hour time slot and will need to build your day around that. You can always skip it in the first part of the tour and come back to it in the afternoon if need be.

The centre of Seville is compact, making it easy to get between the sights on foot. This tour takes in the city's two largest monuments, which both deserve a lengthy visit and together will take up the best part of the day. No visit to Seville, however, is complete without a leisurely walk in the picture-perfect Santa Cruz quarter.

THE CATEDRAL

The obvious place to begin a tour of Seville is at the **Catedral ❶** (www.cate draldesevilla.es; Mon 11am–3pm, Tue–Sat 11am–5pm, Sun 2.30–6pm), on the Plaza del Triunfo. This is the third-largest cathedral in the world after St Peter's in Rome and St Paul's in London.

The cathedral rises from the site of an 1172 mosque. Its bulk was built between 1401 and 1507; the principal structure is Gothic, with later additions in Plateresque and Baroque styles.

It is entered from the south through the **Puerta de San Cristóbal**. A numbered tour leads clockwise around the interior of the building, visiting the 27 chapels that are of varying interest. At the eastern end of the cathedral is the **Capilla Real** (Royal Chapel), the most used and ornate of the side chapels, containing the royal tomb of Fernando III. Fittingly, his remains lie at the feet of the Virgen de los Reyes, the patron saint of Seville. Also here is the tomb of Fernando's queen, Beatriz, and his son Alfonso X (the Wise). On the north side of the cathedral, don't miss the **Capilla de San Antonio** containing Murillo's *Vision of St Antony of Padua*.

The centre of the building is filled by the **Capilla Mayor** (Main Chapel). The

La Giralda and the Catedral   *Tomb of Christopher Columbus*

altarpiece of gilded hardwood contains 36 tableaux of the Old and New Testaments, comprising more than 1,000 figures. Reaching 20 metres (66ft) in height, almost to the roof, it was begun in 1482 by the Flemish sculptor Pieter Dancart and not finished for another 82 years.

On the south side, close to the entrance, is the grand monument to Christopher Columbus. The tomb is carried by four figures representing the kingdoms that made up the Spanish crown at the time of his voyage – Castile, Navarre, Aragón and León. It is not certain that the elaborate sarcophagus contains the remains of the great discoverer, as Columbus's widow had these taken to Santo Domingo in the Dominican Republic, from where they were later moved to Havana's cathedral and then back to Spain: a confusing journey that was poorly documented.

In the southeast corner of the cathedral there are a group of chambers worth entering, notably the **Sacristía de los Cálices**, which has a fine vaulted ceiling and is hung with paintings by Goya, Valdés Leal and Zurbarán.

La Giralda

The high point of the cathedral, however, is its tower, **La Giralda**. This 94-metre (308ft) minaret has been admired ever since its inception on the orders of Moorish ruler Abu-Yaqub Yusuf in 1184.

La Giralda is the finest relic of the Almohad dynasty in Spain. Its beauty reputedly saved it from destruction following the Reconquest in 1248. When negotiating the terms of their surrender, Muslim rulers, tormented by the prospect of the mosque and minaret falling under Christian control, wanted them destroyed. But Alfonso the Wise is said to have refused their plea, threatening to put to death anyone who attempted it.

An earthquake destroyed the tower's original ornamental top in 1356, and it was not until 1558 that it was replaced by the bells and weather vane (*giralda* in Spanish) – a goddess representing Faith by Hernán Ruiz.

The exterior, adorned with typical *sebka* decoration, is in direct contrast to the bland interior, where a series of 35 gently elevated ramps (designed so that horsemen could ride up them) lead visitors to an observation platform at a height of 70 metres (230ft). Archaeological finds and other inter-

Stunning detail in the Salón de los Embajadores, Real Alcázar

esting items are displayed on the landings; they include a pair of 14th-century Mudéjar doors combining Gothic motifs and verses from the Koran.

From the top there are panoramic views of the city, including many patios of old houses, invisible from street level, in the patchwork below.

Off the north side of the cathedral is the **Patio de los Naranjos**, the courtyard of the original mosque, through which you exit. On the way through it you pass the **Puerta del Lagarto** (Gate of the Lizard), named after a life-size wooden alligator hanging from the ceiling, purportedly a replica of a live alligator given to Alfonso X by the Sultan of Egypt.

ARCHIVO GENERAL DE INDIAS

Go around the cathedral to the south, back into Plaza del Triunfo. On this square stands a rather austere Renaissance-style building, formerly the Stock Exchange but now housing the **Archivo General de Indias** ❷ (Mon–Sat 9.30am–5pm, Sun and holidays 10am–2pm; free). It was constructed between 1583 and 1596 by Juan de Herrera, the architect of El Escorial near Madrid. The main points of interest are the central patio, main marble staircase and unusual Cuban wood shelves. The collection comprises some 80 million pages relating to the discovery and colonisation of the New World.

THE ALCÁZAR

The second architectural jewel in Seville is adjacent to the Archivo and across the square from the cathedral. Hidden behind battlemented ochre walls is the **Real Alcázar** ❸ (www.alcazarsevilla. org; daily Apr–Sept 9.30am–7pm, Oct–Mar 9.30am–5pm), the fortress-palace of both Muslim and Christian rulers.

Moroccan invaders built the first fortress on this site in 712. In the 9th century a palace, walls of which are still standing, was added by Amir Abdal-Rahman II. The Moors built additional palaces, though these were still in the fortress style, and added to the gardens during the 11th and 12th centuries.

Following the Reconquest, the Catholic Monarchs established a court here, and King Don Pedro (known as Pedro the Cruel) built a luxurious Mudéjar-style palace on this site in 1364. It was renovated in the 16th century by Carlos V.

The entrance is through the **Puerta del León**, marked by a heraldic lion, in the original 11th-century walls. Beyond is the **Patio del León**, a former assembly ground, at the far end of which three arches lead into the Patio de la Montería, the inner courtyard. Before proceeding through here, take the passage in the far-left corner to reach the **Sala de Justicia**, considered to be the first example of Mudéjar-style architecture, built by Alfonso XI, and beyond that the lovely **Patio del Yeso** (Courtyard of Plasterwork), which formed part of the 12th-century Almohad palace.

The sculpted Alcázar gardens

Regaining the Patio del León, proceed through the arches to the **Patio de la Montería**, faced by the ornate facade of Don Pedro's Palace. On the right-hand side is the **Sala del Almirante** (Admiral's Hall), containing historical memorabilia and 18th-century paintings depicting the overthrow of the Moors.

In the adjacent **Chapel** (which has a fine 16th-century coffered ceiling), the altar painting has a nautical theme appropriate to the rooms, which were specifically built for the planning of naval expeditions. A figure hidden in the Virgen de los Navegantes' skirts is supposed to be Christopher Columbus.

The main entrance to the part of the Alcázar known as el Palacio de Rey Don Pedro is surmounted by an inscription to Pedro the Cruel. Inside, turn left. The dog-leg vestibule (typical of Arab architecture but here also used to confuse would-be assassins) leads into the **Patio de las Doncellas** (Maid's Courtyard). It has a compact grace and quiet beauty. Koranic inscriptions ('None but Allah Conquers') combine with Mudéjar motifs.

Notable in the apartments is the magnificent **Salón de los Embajadores** (Ambassador's Hall), effectively the throne room, dating from the 11th-century palace. It has an intricately carved and gilded dome (15th century), resting on a frieze of alternating castles and lions, and exquisite geometric and floral carvings on the walls. Beyond is the small **Patio de las Muñecas** (Courtyard of the Dolls), a private family chamber, named after two tiny faces, eroded but still visible, in the decoration on the columns, and the **Cuarto del Príncipe** (Prince's Suite), named after the son of the Catholic Monarchs, who was born here in 1478.

THE ALCÁZAR'S GARDENS

Behind the Alcázar are extensive **gardens**, a complex of patios, pools and pavilions. Nearest to the Salones de Carlos V is the Garden of El Estanque ('The Pool'), Renaissance in style but set around a rectangular pool that once irrigated the Moors' orchards. From here the **Gallery of El Etrusco** (1612–21), with views over the Garden of Las Damas ('The Ladies'), follows the course of the **Almohad Wall**. Evening concerts are held in the gardens in summer.

SANTA CRUZ

Exiting the Alcázar you step into the Patio de Banderas. Turn right immediately and take the short tunnel leading into Calle Judería. You are now in the Santa Cruz quarter, a cluster of narrow picturesque streets and squares, white houses, secret azulejo-decorated patios, window grilles and flower pots. The delight here is taking things slowly and following your nose to wander off the route every now and then to peer down alleyways and into little squares.

Las Teresas flaunting its wares

Turn right down Judería until you come to the wall of the Alcázar. Turn left up Calle Agua (or Callejón de Agua), following the wall until you reach the corner. On the way you pass an excellent restaurant, the **Corral del Agua,** see ❶. Cross Plaza Alfaro diagonally to find yourself in **Plaza de Santa Cruz ❹**, the true heart of the quarter and the site of Los Gallos, one of the best known of the traditional flamenco venues in town (see page 121).

Go straight across the square and up Calle Mezquita, which skirts Plaza de los Refinadores with its monument to Don Juan Tenorio, the notorious (fictional) seducer and rake of Seville invented by José Zorrilla. Turn left down Calle Cruces. Continue across the triangular Plaza de las Cruces and you will strike Calle Ximenez de Enciso. Turn left here. No. 22 on this street is the **Centro de Interpretación Judería de Sevilla ❺** (Calle Ximénez de Enciso 22; www.juderiadesevilla.es; daily 11am–7pm), an exhibition about Santa Cruz's Jewish history.

If you are ready for drinks and tapas, try **Las Teresas ❷**, on the next street on the left (going back towards Plaza Santa Cruz). Alternatively, go down Ximenez de Enciso and turn right on to Calle Mesón del Moro and left down Calle Mateos Gago, where you will find the **Cervezeria Giralda ❸**, a well-known bar and restaurant.

At the end of the street you will find yourself in Plaza Virgen de los Reyes, which connects (on the left) to your starting point, the Plaza del Triunfo.

Food and Drink

❶ CORRAL DEL AGUA

Calle Agua, 6; tel: 954-224 841; www.corraldelagua.es; L and D; €€€
This elegant restaurant occupies a restored 18th-century house that centres on a pleasant patio filled with potted plants. On midweek evenings there's live music: classical Spanish guitar on Tuesdays and Wednesdays and jazz, bolero or swing on Thursdays. Traditional Andalucían dishes.

❷ LAS TERESAS

Calle Santa Teresa 2; tel: 954-213 069; www.lasteresas.es; L and D; €
If you don't want a formal meal, this is a straightforward neighbourhood bar with walls crammed with photos and memorabilia and a few tables outside. Above all, it has an excellent selection of tapas.

❸ CERVECERIA GIRALDA

Mateos Gago 1; tel: 954-228 250; cerveceriagiralda.com; L and D; €€
With its columns, arches and ornate tileworks, this is one of Seville's classic tapas bars. Full meals are also served. Reservation advised in busy periods.

Pedestrians navigate the Guadalquivir

SEVILLE ALONG THE RIVERSIDE

The numerous sights outside the city centre are linked up here by a pleasant walk along the banks of the Guadalquivir, the navigable river on which Seville's historic prosperity was founded.

DISTANCE: 4km (2.5 miles)
TIME: 1 day
START: Plaza de la Encarnación
END: Plaza de España
POINTS TO NOTE: If you have time to do some in-depth visiting and want to cross the river to Triana and the Isla de Cartuja, you may want to spread this route over two days.

Seville would be unthinkable without its watery artery, the Guadalquivir River. In Roman days, trading vessels used the waterway to reach the wharfs of the city; later, fleets returning from the New World unloaded their cargoes of gold and silver here. The river is now used for leisure rather than commerce, but it remains one of Seville's main attractions.

FROM LAS SETAS DE SEVILLA TO THE RIVER

The route begins away from the river in the Plaza de la Encarnacion, site of Seville's newest attraction, **Las Setas de**

Sevilla ① or Metropol Parasol (https://setasdesevilla.com; daily 10am–11pm), a curvaceous high-level viewing platform described as the largest wooden structure in the world. The bar at the top, **El Balcón de las Setas**, also serves tapas – see ①.

Take the road west towards the river, which begins as Calle Laraña but continues as Martin Villa, Campana and finally Calle Alfonso XII, until you come to a park on the left. Here you'll find the fine arts museum, the **Museo de Bellas Artes** ② (www.museosdeandalucia.es; Tue–Sat 9am–9pm, Sun 9am–3pm), housed in the 17th-century Convento de la Merced Calzada. It is considered the second most important art gallery in Spain after the Prado in Madrid. Inside are works by El Greco, Goya, Murillo, Zurbarán, Velázquez and Valdés Leal, among others.

Behind the museum, Calle Pedro de Toro leads you to the Plaza de Armas shopping and leisure centre, a converted railway station. Turn left down Marqués de Paradas and right on Calle Reyes Católicos to reach the river.

PUENTE DE ISABEL II

You are now at the end of the lovely **Puente de Isabel II** ❸, with a statue of the famous bullfighter Manolete

(1917–47) at its end. The route stays on this side of the river, but on the opposite bank is a whole other Seville if you have time to explore it another day. Immediately across the bridge is **Triana**,

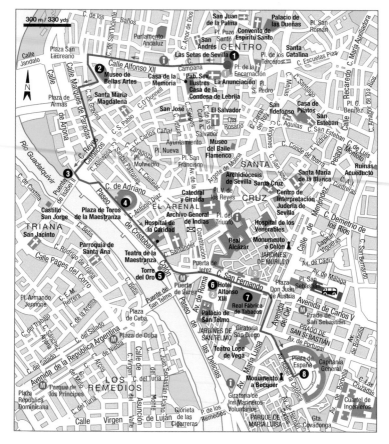

The Real Fábrica de Tabacos was built in 1750

the traditional gypsy quarter and one of the homes of flamenco music. Triana is also renowned for its ceramics. North of Triana is the Isla de la Cartuja, site of Seville's Expo 92 World Fair, and of the Isla Mágica theme park.

For now, turn left at the bridge along Paseo de Cristobal Colón (the Spanish name for Christopher Columbus). On your left is the **Plaza de Toros de la Maestranza** ❹ (www.realmaestranza. com; daily Nov–Mar 9.30am–7pm, Apr–Oct 9.30am–9pm, 9.30am–3pm on days of bullfights), which is more than just a bullring; it is a legendry venue for lovers of *la corrida*. Rather than being circular, it is polygonal and can accommodate more than 13,000 spectators. It can be visited on a 55-minute guided tour (in both Spanish and English).

Continuing along the Paseo you come to Seville's opera house, the Teatro de la Maestranza and then, on the other side of the road, the **Torre del Oro** ❺ (Mon–Fri 9.30am–6.45pm, Sat and Sun 10.30am–6.45pm) which, despite being much shorter, is almost as much of a landmark in Seville as La Giralda. Dating from 1220, it was built outside the city walls as a watchtower. It also served a defensive purpose by anchoring a chain that stretched across the river. At other times it was used to store gold brought back from the Americas, and as a prison. The round top and spire were added in the 18th century.

Cruises depart from here to discover a short stretch of the Guadalquivir River that flows across Andalucía from the Sierra de Cazorla to the Gulf of Cádiz. It is the only navigable river in Spain.

Fork left at the tower up Calle Almirante Lobo to the Plaza Puerta de Jerez, on which stands the palatial **Hotel Alfonso XIII** ❻ (see page 106), built in imitation of the Seville patio style for the 1929 Ibero-American Exhibition and named in honour of the monarch who was forced to abdicate in 1931 to make way for a republic. The hotel has elegant salons around a central courtyard and many ornamental flourishes. If you're feeling flush, you might want to treat yourself to a meal here, in the **San Fernando** restaurant, see ❷, or a drink in the Art Deco American-style bar. For a more wallet-friendly option, try **100 Montaditos** ❸, further down the road on the opposite side.

TOBACCO FACTORY

Next door to the hotel, on Calle San Fernando, is the **Real Fábrica de Tabacos** ❼ (Royal Tobacco Factory), a reminder of one of the most cherished discoveries of the New World. By the 18th century, when this vast and handsome, if austere, factory building was erected, tobacco was being chewed and smoked all over Europe. Much of it was supplied by the 3,000 female workers, *cigarreras*,

The exquisite, colonnaded Plaza de España

who worked here rolling cigarettes on their thighs. They were immortalised by Bizet in the mythical figure of Carmen in his opera of the same name. The factory is now part of Seville University.

THE PARQUE MARÍA LUISA

Turn right at the Plaza Don Juan de Austria on Avenida del Cid (going back towards the river) and at the next roundabout (Glorieta de San Diego) turn left on Avenida Isabel la Católica. You are now in the vast **Parque María Luisa** (daily 8am–10pm, until midnight in summer), the former gardens of the long vanished Palacio de San Telmo and the site of Seville's Ibero-American Exhibition in 1929.

To your left is the most eye-catching remnant of the exhibition and one of Seville's greatest monuments, the **Plaza de España ❸**, which was used as a backdrop in one of the *Star Wars* films. The extraordinary semi-circular building half enclosing it took 15 years to build and functioned as the Spanish pavilion. Its towers were inspired by the cathedral at Santiago de Compostela in Galicia, and the elaborately tiled panels below the colonnade depict the Spanish provinces, running in alphabetical order from left to right. The moat has little bridges decorated with extraordinary *azulejo*-covered balustrades. There are rowing boats for hire on the 515-metre/yd long canal, an agreeable way to mark the end of the route.

Food and Drink

❶ EL BALCON DE LAS SETAS
Plaza de la Encarnación; tel: 954-217 225; http://elbalcondelassetas.es; tapas; €€
Situated on the viewing platform of Las Setas de Sevilla, with stunning panoramas. Its speciality is *carrillada*: pork flavoured with wine and spices.

❷ SAN FERNANDO (HOTEL ALFONSO XIII)
Calle San Fernando, 2; tel: 954-917 000; www.hotel-alfonsoxiii-seville.com; R, L and D; €€€
The restaurant of Seville's top hotel, frequented by visiting celebrities, is in the

colonnaded courtyard. It is an elegant place to eat lunch or dinner, and on Sunday mornings it puts on Seville's best brunch, to the accompaniment of live piano music.

❸ 100 MONTADITOS
Calle San Fernando 29; tel: 954-914 118; spain.100montaditos.com; B, L and D; €
This hugely successful Spanish franchise chain is useful to know about. It emanates from Huelva and while its bars don't have age and character, they are convenient places to eat. The company's speciality is the mini-sandwich (*montadito*), which comes in a number of varieties.

Doñana National Park

DOÑANA NATIONAL PARK AND HUELVA

Southwest of Seville is one of Europe's largest national parks – a seaside expanse of dunes and marshes with a rich wildlife population. This drive combines nature spotting with an enjoyable history lesson about the discovery of the New World.

DISTANCE: 275km (170 miles)
TIME: 2 days
START & END: Seville
POINTS TO NOTE: If you want to visit Doñana National Park on an organised tour, you'll need to arrange this in advance. For more information, see donanavisitas.es (tel: 959-430 432) or discoveringdonana.com (tel: 620-964 369).

It is not far from Seville to the Portuguese border, but between the two is one of Europe's most famous national parks. This trip passes through it and then continues on to visit sites connected with explorer Christopher Columbus, before looping back to the point of departure.

SEVILLE TO PARQUE NACIONAL DE DOÑANA

Leave **Seville** ❶ on the A49 motorway heading west towards Huelva. Turn off for Almonte. When the motorway comes to an end, continue on the A483 to **El**

Rocío ❷, which is dominated by the **Ermita del Rocío**, the focus for one of Spain's largest and most ecstatic annual pilgrimages, the Romería del Rocío. At Whitsun (Pentecost), this sleepy backwater is transformed by festivity, overrun with up to a million costumed, singing revellers, riding in flower-filled carriages. Excitement centres on a tiny wooden effigy of the Virgin Mary, Nuestra Senora del Rocío, that is kept above the church altar and revered for a miraculous legend about her discovery.

Continue along the A483 towards Matalascañas, heading for the sea. Before you get there, you enter **Parque Nacional de Doñana**, Spain's largest nature reserve. The heart of the reserve is a river delta that periodically floods, creating seasonal wetlands and a system of shifting and evolving dunes. This combination of ecosystems provides a precious habitat for a huge diversity of birds and mammals, including many endangered species.

A signpost indicates the national park visitor centre of **El Acebuche** ❸ (daily 8am–3pm and 4–7pm, later closing in summer). There is an exhibition about

Monasterio de La Rábida

the flora and fauna of the reserve here and you can follow two nature trails around nearby lagoons. To protect its fragile environment, access to the interior of the Doñana is restricted to organised tours, which can be booked either in person or, better still, in advance.

COLUMBUS TERRITORY

Along the coast
Return to the A483 and continue until you strike the sea. To the left is the resort of Matalascañas, which has various beach restaurants (*chirringuitos*) to choose from in the summer season. A short way back from the sea is the bar-restaurant **Acebrón**, see ❶.

If you are not going into Matalascañas to eat, turn right on the A494, which follows the coast. At Mazagón take the left fork, the N442, and turn off on to the A5025 to visit the monastery of La Rabida.

Monasterio de La Rábida and Muelle de las Carabelas
Hidden by the surrounding oil refineries, the Franciscan **Monasterio de La Rábida** ❹ (www.monasteriodela rabida.com; Tue–Sat 10am–1pm and 4–6.15pm, until 7pm in summer, Sun year-round 10.45am–1pm) is a tranquil sanctuary. It was at La Rábida that Columbus met Friar Juan Pérez, the former priest of Queen Isabel, who intervened on Columbus's behalf and persuaded the Spanish monarchy to

back his expedition. Murals depicting the events of 1492 and headset commentary in English vividly bring to life Columbus's time at the monastery.

The visit includes the cloister, set around a Moorish courtyard, the early 15th-century church (where one of Columbus's locally recruited captains, Martín Alonso Pinzón, is buried) and the chapel where the explorer is thought to have prayed before his departure.

From the upstairs chapter house, in which much of the voyage was planned, there is a view of the river and a reproduction of the 15th-century harbour, **Muelle de las Carabelas** (Tue–Sun mid-June–mid-Sept 10am–9pm, mid-Sept -mid-June 9.30am–7.30pm), where there are life-size replicas of the maiden flotilla that can be visited. The surprisingly small dimensions of the wooden vessels and the confined living quarters highlight the remarkable bravery and determination of the crew.

Palos de la Frontera
Further along the A5025 is **Palos de la Frontera**. This was a sizeable port in August 1492 when the tiny fleet set sail for the New World. It has since clogged up with silt from the Tinto estuary, so Columbus's precise departure point is hidden under clay. A great source of local pride is the town's status as home of the Pinzón brothers, who captained caravels *Nina* and *Pinta* on the expedition (Columbus himself captained the *Santa María*). There is a museum at the Pinzón

Palos de la Frontera   *Moguer looking festive*

family home (on Calle Cristóbal Colón) and a monument to Martín Alonso Pinzón in the central square, marking the spot where the royal order for the 'Enterprise of the Indies' was declared.

Moguer

Continue on the A5025 and then the A494 into **Moguer ⑤**, which also claims a connection with Columbus as the recruiting ground for much of the crew. It is also home to the 14th-century **Monasterio de Santa Clara** (www.monasteriodesantaclara.com; Tue–Sat guided tours 10.30am, 11.30am, 12.30pm, 5.30pm and 6.30pm, Sun 10.30am and 11.30am), where Columbus prayed through the night in thanks for his safe return. The town retains a distinctly Moorish feel with its whitewashed walls and dead ends. Buildings of interest include the graceful 18th-century **Ayuntamiento** (Mon–Fri 11am–2pm), which has a fine patio, on Plaza del Cabildo. Opposite is a statue of local poet Juan Ramón Jiménez, winner of the 1956 Nobel Prize for Literature. If you're hungry, try **La Parrala ②**.

HUELVA

After Moguer the A494 meets the A472. At this point, make a detour into **Huelva city ⑥**, only 13km (8 miles) from the main route and a good place to stop for the night (see page 107). The city's historic centre, which withstood the 1755 Lisbon earthquake and remains elegant and proud. The Baroque **Catedral de la Merced** dominates a shady plaza (off Paseo Buenos Aires), which has the grand but slightly edgy feel of a South American plaza – a reminder of Huelva's intercontinental influence. Trade with the New World brought wealth, though in time most of this was absorbed by Seville. A smart pedestrianised shopping district runs south of the central **Plaza de las Monjas**, parallel to Gran Vía. At the eastern end of this main thoroughfare, the **Museo de Huelva** (Tue–Sat 9am–8pm, Sun 9am–3pm) sheds light on the enigmatic Tartessos civilisation, which is thought to have centred on Huelva.

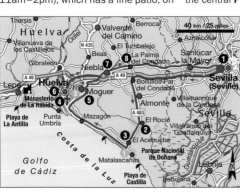

NIEBLA

Take the A472 towards Seville, crossing over the

A49 motorway. You enter the next town, **Niebla** ❼, over a restored Roman bridge. The red oxides that tinge the soil and waters of the Río Tinto can be seen in the crimson walls of the town. This is more than a colourful detail: it is testament to the mining industry on which Niebla's fortunes were founded.

The town is still enclosed by walls punctuated by 46 towers and various gateways, and incorporating a magnificent 15th century *alcázar*. At its centre are the attractive **Plaza Santa Maria** and the 10th-century church of the same name, which has a minaret, intricate gates and a mihrab testifying to its conversion from a mosque in the 13th century.

The town has several other ancient churches. The **Iglesia de San Martín** incorporates evidence of Visigothic origins, Muslim conversion and Mudéjar remodelling, reflecting the history of Niebla itself.

LA PALMA DEL CONDADO

Stay on the A472 to the next town, **La Palma del Condado** ❽. Many of the taller buildings within easy flying distance of the Doñana mudflats have been occupied by nesting storks, and La Palma's attractive 18th-century church, San Juan Bautista, is no exception. A tangle of twigs tops its ornate blue baroque tower like a chimney brush. This is Huelva's wine-growing region, and it has been planted with vines for centuries. Of the three del Condado (county) towns – La Palma, Rociana and Bollullos, the last (south of La Palma) offers cavernous, high-ceilinged bodegas with trestle tables to accommodate noisy wine-tastings. Typically the region's wines, derived from the local Zalema grape, are amber-coloured, nutty olorosos, similar to dark sherry. However, in recent years, wine-makers have been switching to fruity young whites, which go well with the local seafood.

You can stay on the A472 to reach Seville via Sanlúcar la Mayor, but a much faster option is to take the A493 spur form La Palma to the motorway – the A49 – and return to the city that way.

The rooftops of Osuna

FOUR TOWNS: CARMONA, ÉCIJA, OSUNA AND ANTEQUERA

Inland Andalucía is dotted with handsome historic towns that are easily overlooked. This route connects up four of the best – Carmona, Écija, Osuna and Antequera – in a tour using mainly fast backroads.

DISTANCE: 193 km (120 miles)
TIME: 1 day
START: Seville
END: Antequera
POINTS TO NOTE: This part of Andalucía gets hot, even outside the summer months. Wear a hat, stay in the shade where possible and drink plenty of water.

This route takes in some of the towns that modern transport would rather pass by at high velocity. It can serve as an indirect way to get from Seville to Málaga, and can also be adapted to provide a scenic link between Seville and Córdoba.

CARMONA

From **Seville ❶**, take the A4 (E5) motorway towards Córdoba to reach **Carmona ❷**, just 20km (12 miles) east. It sits like a beacon on top of the only hill on an otherwise unrelenting plain, a position that has given it strategic importance during its 5,000-year history. The town declined after the

Romans left, but when the Moors reached Carmona in 713 they brought renewed growth and prosperity. The Moors' reign ended in 1247 when King Fernando III of Castile reconquered Carmona.

Follow the signs into the centre of town and park outside the walls, as near to the **Puerta de Sevilla** (which looks like a miniature castle) as you can. This gateway-cum-*alcázar* accommodates the tourist office.

Walk through the gateway and you are in the old quarter. At the far end of town is another gateway, the **Puerta de Córdoba,** remarkably intact considering its age (originally 2nd-century, with Moorish and Baroque additions) and the castle, the Alcazar del Rey don Pedro I (now a parador, see page 107). There is a pleasant little restaurant near here, **La Yedra**, see ❶.

When you have finished with the centre, walk or drive to the Roman ruins (on the Seville side of town), the **Conjunto Arqueológico de Carmona** (Apr–June Tue–Sat 9am–9pm, Sun 9am–3pm, July–Mar daily 9am–3pm), where a Roman amphitheatre, necropolis and museum can be visited. The necropolis

is the largest Roman burial ground outside Rome and is complete with a crematorium (its walls still discoloured by the fire), a large numbers of small paupers' tombs and some much grander edifices.

ÉCIJA

Resume along the motorway you left earlier and drive on to **Écija** ❸. The town stands on the Rio Genil, a tributary of the Guadalquivir, which makes its way here from the distant Sierra Nevada near Granada. Unlike most Andalucían towns, Écija sits in a valley bowl rather than on a hill, and therefore has no summer breeze to relieve the relentless summer heat. Little wonder that it is known as 'the frying pan of Spain'.

The **Museo Histórico Municipal** (Calle Cánovas del Castillo; museo.ecija.es; June–Sept Tue–Fri 10am–2.30pm,

Sat 10am–2pm and 8–10pm, Sun 10am–3pm, Oct–May Tue–Fri 10am–1.30pm and 4.30–6.30pm, Sat 10am–2pm and 5.30–8pm, Sun 10am–3pm; free) has some interesting Roman finds, while the **Iglesia de Santa María** (southwest of the Plaza Major) has a Mudéjar patio filled with archaeological artefacts. The covered market is worth dipping into, and Calle Caballeros (north of the main square) has several rambling and ornate merchants' houses, including the **Palacio de Peñaflor**, with an unusual curved balcony. The town is littered with crumbling church towers, all of which echo Seville's Giralda. To eat, try **Las Ninfas Gastrobar** ❷.

OSUNA

Here you leave the motorway. Cut due south from Écija on the A351 to

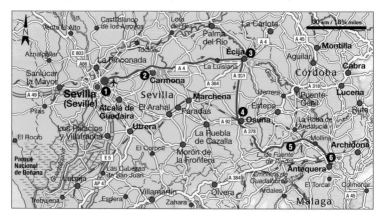

Palacio de Peñaflor balcony

Osuna ❹, a handsome and harmonious town with a large collection of merchant and aristocratic houses, reflecting its history as the seat of the dukes of Osuna. There is an imitation of La Giralda built into a grand facade on the Calle San Pedro, next door to the grandly baroque **Palacio del Marqués de La Gomera** (now a hotel, see page 107).

The true monumental centre, used as many a film location, is up a steep hill above the town, around Plazas del Duque and España. Looking down on the town is the church of **La Colegiata de Santa María** (including a ducal sepulchre). Next to it is the 16th-century turreted **Universidad de Osuna**, the former university, with its blue and white turrets. Below is the **Museo Arqueologico** (Tue–Sun May–Sept 10am–1.30pm and 5–7pm, July and Aug morning only, Oct–Apr 10am–1.30pm and 3.30–6.30pm; free) in the Torre del Agua, a 12th-century Almohad tower refurbished by the Knights of Calatrava.

FUENTE DE PIEDRA

Follow the signs out of Osuna on to the little road to Martin de la Jarra (A378). Turn left for Sierra de Yeguas and here take the A7279 going east to Fuente de Piedra. The plains north of Antequera, it has to be said, aren't all that interesting, but they do have one place of interest, a salty lake, the **Laguna de la Fuente de Piedra ❺**. This is the largest natural lake in Andalucía, famous for its colony of flamingos – although you'll be lucky to see any without binoculars. There is a visitor centre (www.visitasfuentepiedra.es; daily Apr–Sep 10am–2pm and 5–7pm, Oct–Mar 10am–2pm and 4–6pm) with a lookout point on a rise 1km (0.6 miles) from the town.

ANTEQUERA

Pick up the motorway at Fuente de Piedra and drive south, following the signs into the centre of **Antequera ❻**, a town standing on a rich, fertile plain.

The natural place to begin sightseeing is the **Plaza San Sebastián**, on which stands a 16th-century church of the same name with a Baroque-Mudéjar tower and a Renaissance facade, an example of the town's architectural richness.

Behind the tourist office, a straight street, Calle Zapateros, leads uphill away from the noise and traffic, around a dogleg to the monumental gateway of the **Arco de los Gigantes** (Giants' Arch), dedicated in 1585 to Felipe II. Through the arch you step into the **Plaza Santa María**, overlooked by the Renaissance

El Torcal

In the hills behind Antequera is one of Andalucía's foremost beauty spots, El Torcal (tel: 952-243 324; www.torcaldeante quera.com; daily Apr–Oct 10am–7pm, Nov–Mar 10am–5pm), a collection of limestone outcrops sculpted into abstract forms by erosion over millions of years.

Dolmen de Viera

church of **Real Colegiata de Santa María la Mayor** (Mon and Wed–Sun 10am–6pm, Tue 2–6pm). One side of the square looks over the Roman ruins of the **Termas Romanas** (Roman Baths), and access to the Muslim fortress of the **Alcazaba** (same opening times as Santa María la Mayor) is also off the square. At the top of the Alcazaba, standing proud above the city, is the keep to which a belfry was added in the 16th century.

On the way downhill from this complex of monuments is the **Museo de la Ciudad de Antequera** (Tue–Fri 10am–2pm and 4.30–6.30pm, Sat 9.30am–2pm and 4.30–6.30pm, Sun 9.30am–2pm; free Sun), housed in the Baroque **Palacio de Nájera**. Although it has eight galleries of art and ecclesiastical silverware, most visitors are drawn to the archaeology section and to one piece in particular, the **Efebo de Antequera**. This 1.5-metre (5ft) high bronze figure of a youth has been described as the most beautiful Roman find in Spain, even without the glass eyes that once filled its hollow sockets. It was cast in the 1st century AD and probably served as a lamp or candle holder.

Dolmens

On the outskirts of town, on the way out towards Granada, are three massive prehistoric dolmens (burial mounds). Two of these, the **Dolmen de Menga** and the **Dolmen de Viera** (Tue–Sat 9–6pm, Sun 9am–3pm; free), stand together in a park created around them. Menga is the oldest, dating from 2500 BC, and also the most impressive: an assembly of 31 stones, the largest weighing 180 tonnes.

The third dolmen, **Romeral** (same opening times), stands alone in a peaceful location behind a small industrial estate. Dating from around 1800 BC, it is the most recent, but also the most architecturally interesting.

There is a good restaurant near the roundabout beside the Dolmen de Romeral, inevitably called **Los Dolmenes 3**.

Bodega tour in Jerez de la Frontera

COSTA DE LA LUZ

This drive down southern Spain's Atlantic seaboard takes in the famous wine city of Jerez de la Frontera and romantic Cádiz, one of the world's most ancient ports, before ending up on a windy headland with a view of Africa.

DISTANCE: 195km (122 miles)
TIME: 2 days
START: Jerez de la Frontera
END: Tarifa
POINTS TO NOTE: Both days of this tour can be done from the same base if you want to avoid changing hotel. Either way, vibrant Cádiz makes a good place to bed down in between days one and two.

South of Seville, occupying the south-western corner of Andalucía, is the province of Cádiz. Its coast is officially called the Costa de la Luz – the coast of light – referring to the quality of sunshine, often reflecting off the glittering ocean, and the golden sands of its shores. Strong ocean winds blow off the Atlantic, which have saved the beaches here from overdevelopment, and you may get to enjoy the inspirational sunset all by yourself. The other pleasure you can look forward to is eating the freshest fish and seafood, washed down with a crisp local sherry.

JEREZ DE LA FRONTERA

Begin by visiting **Jerez de la Frontera ❶**, which is easily reached by train or car from Seville. The name Jerez has been anglicised as sherry, an indication of the city's main industry – although it would be wrong to think only in terms of the dark, sweet wines beloved of English drawing rooms. The preferred drink of Andalucía, and Jerez's emblematic product, is fino, a strong dry white wine. Several of the major bodegas (wine producers) in Jerez are open to visitors. The largest is **González Byass** (Calle Manuel Maria González 12; tel: 956-357 016; www.bodegastiopepe. com). Its cellar, La Concha, located near the cathedral and Alcázar, was designed by Gustave Eiffel. The fanciest is **Bodegas Tradición** (Calle Cordobeses 3; tel: 956-168 628; www.bodegastradicion. es), which has an exquisite private art collection. Near to the equestrian school is **Bodegas Sandeman** (Calle Pizarro 10; tel: 675-647 177; www.sandeman.com), where the guides wear the black cape and *caballero* hat of its trademark Don. For any visit, it is a good idea to book ahead.

Plaza del Cabildo, Sanlúcar de Barrameda

Jerez is also famous for the horses of the **Real Escuela Andaluza del Arte Ecuestre** (Royal Andalucían School of Equestrian Art; tel: 956-319 635; www.realescuela.org; daily 10am–2pm), where dressage training to a soundtrack of Spanish guitar music can be watched on a stables tour, which also includes entry to the museum. The horses give a polished performance in the arena on Tuesdays and Thursdays at noon. In May, Jerez holds a showy horse fair: a must for anyone with equestrian interest.

The other two sights to see are the Gothic-Baroque cathedral and the *alcázar* (daily 9.30am–2.30pm, until 5.30pm Mon–Fri July–Sept), which incorporates an exquisite mosque, attractive gardens and Arab baths lit by starry skylights. An 18th-century palace has been built within the medieval walls.

There are endless places to eat and drink in Jerez, but to enjoy tapas in a dappled courtyard, seek out **Alboronía** .

SANLÚCAR DE BARRAMEDA

From Jerez, take the motorway (A480) northwest to **Sanlúcar de Barrameda** ❷, situated on the estuary of the Río Guadalquivir. Once Seville's main port, Sanlúcar shared in its New World spoils; historical wealth accounts for its elegant architecture, focusing on the palm-lined Plaza del Cabildo. This is another wine town: it specialises in manzanilla wine, considered to be more delicate than sherry and deriving its distinct flavour

from the salty, humid conditions that prevail here. Sanlúcar's restored aristocratic residence, **Palacio Duques de Medina Sidonia** (Wed and Thu at noon, Sun at 11.30am and noon), contains an excellent cafeteria for a spot of tea, see ❷. Trips also depart for Doñana National Park (Viajes Doñana; tel: 956-362 540; www.viajesdonana.es) on the opposite bank of the river. If you happen to visit in August, the town's fiesta includes horse racing along a stretch of the beach.

EL PUERTO DE SANTA MARÍA

A straight main road, the A2001 leads to **El Puerto de Santa María** ❸, a thriving port near the mouth of the River Guadalete. On summer evenings locals and visitors tend to converge on the Ribera del Marisco, to enjoy the sociable atmosphere and first-rate seafood.

The town is ringed by yet more wineries, including the vast Bodegas Osborne (tel: 956-869 100; www.bodegas-osborne.com), the brand advertised by the iconic black bull, whose silhouette is a familiar feature on roadside hills throughout Andalucía. El Puerto's good beaches are a few kilometres west of town, becoming less crowded the further they are from the centre. The best of them is **Playa Santa Catalina**.

CÁDIZ

There are two options for the next leg of the tour. One is to leave your car in El

Learning dressage   *Cádiz's Castillo de San Sebastián*

Puerto de Santa María and take a round trip to **Cádiz ❹** by boat across the bay to avoid traffic jams. Otherwise, follow the signs along the motorway into Cádiz and park as close to the centre as you can – or at your hotel if you're overnighting here.

The port city of Cádiz is thought to have been founded by the Phoenicians and has enjoyed a busy naval and mercantile history. It still has the feel of a fortified outpost, almost entirely surrounded by the sea, anchored to its province by a finger of land and a high bridge carrying traffic across the bay.

The city's famous carnival is held in February or March, when Cádiz hosts 10 days of music and revelry. This is the most spectacular carnival celebration in mainland Spain and includes costumed parades and a competition for troubadours singing satirical songs.

Orientation

Despite the confusing jumble of backstreets, it is impossible to get lost in Cádiz, which requires inquisitive zigzag wandering. The city is no more than 2km (1.2 miles) wide in any given direction, so whichever way you walk the ocean soon reappears. The imposing **Puerta de Tierra** divides the old town from more modern development along the deep Atlantic beaches.

On the western side of the peninsula is **Barrio de la Viña**, a fisherman's quarter where inhabitants can often be seen collecting crabs by the causeway to the military islet of **Castillo de San Sebastián**. They moor their boats in the small **Playa de la Caleta**.

Plazas, towers and museums

Further on round the seafront are the **Castillo de Santa Catalina** and two

Vejer de la Frontera

shady parks, **Parque Genovés** and the **Alameda de Apodaca**. Set back from the sea is the largest, leafiest square, the **Plaza de España**, from where streets delve into a warren of atmospheric, if slightly seedy, nooks and crannies. A short walk west of here in Plaza de Mina is the **Museo de Cádiz** (Tue–Sat 9am–9pm, Sun 9am–3pm), boasting a fine collection of art, including works by Zurbarán and Murillo, as well as Roman relics from Baelo Claudia.

Cádiz entered a golden era in the 18th century, when it overtook Seville as the centre for transatlantic trade. The city's most impressive architecture dates from this time, including its watchtowers, the highest being **Torre Tavira** (www.torretavira.com; daily May–Sept 10am–8pm, Oct–Apr 10am–6pm), noted now for its camera obscura, and grand avenues such as **Calle Ancha** ('Broad Street').

Prosperity in turn produced a discursive middle class, who earned the city a liberal reputation. The **Museo de las Cortes de Cádiz** (Tue–Fri 9am–6pm, Sat–Sun 9am–2pm; free) records the short-lived democratic constitution of 1812, declared at the Oratorio San Felipe Neri next door.

Two cathedrals

The vast **Catedral Nueva**, fronted by a wide, open, pedestrianised plaza, is one of the largest cathedrals in Spain and took 122 years to complete (1716–1838), hence the mix of Baroque and neoclassical design. Entered separately from the Plaza de la Catedral, a spiral climb inside one of the bell towers, Torre del Reloj, offers a 360° panorama.

In the shadow of the 'new' cathedral, **Barrio del Populo** (the heart of 13th-century Cádiz, with three surviving medieval gates) is home to the old one. The **Iglesia Santa Cruz** was virtually demolished by the British in 1596 and later rebuilt. A short walk across **Plaza de San Juan de Dios** leads to the harbour; Cádiz is a significant port for cruise liners and commercial vessels. The docks are also the departure point for a trip across the bay to El Puerto de Santa María (to return to your car, if you've left it there)

It would be criminal to visit Cádiz without sampling some of its fish and seafood, fresh from its ocean larder. The best place to indulge is **El Faro de Cádiz** ❺, a restaurant and high-class tapas bar.

VEJER DE LA FRONTERA

Head south from Cadiz on the A48 motorway past Chiclana de la Frontera and turn off for **Vejer de la Frontera** ❺, a white town with the ultimate sea view. Vejer's elevated isolation is impressive, like a suspended white-iced wedding cake looming above the road. Behind Moorish gates a maze of steep and twisting alleyways lead to the Castillo and the 16th-century church of Divino Salvador, built around the minaret of a

mosque. The central Plaza de España is reminiscent of Seville, with its orange trees and *azulejo*-decorated fountains.

From Vejer take the A2230 towards the sea and turn left onto the A2233 through Zahora. A short spur takes you to **Cabo Trafalgar** ❻ (Cape of Trafalgar). The sea off this point was the scene of Admiral Nelson's famous obliteration of the combined fleets of France and Spain on 21 October 1805. Despite being vastly outnumbered, the British fleet won the day through their skill and experience, though Nelson himself was fatally wounded. The battle was decisive in ensuring Britain's supremacy at sea for the next 100 years. A lighthouse topping a breezy, dune-smothered spit marks the spot.

The A2233 takes you next through **Los Caños de Meca** ❼, tucked under pine-clad hills. It was once a hippie resort and an uninhibited mood encourages discreet naturists, who swim from the smaller southern bay. A few hotels and restaurants are scattered along a ridge of sandstone cliffs, with hidden caves and two stunning golden beaches nestled beneath. This spot is captivating at sunset, when the sun sinks into the ocean behind the nearby Cape.

An attractive drive leads up through the umbrella pines of the **Parque Natural de la Breña y Marismas de Barbate** and down to the town of **Barbate**, a fishing harbour renowned for its bluefin tuna. Seafood eateries dot the otherwise unremarkable Paseo Maritimo.

Further down the coast is **Zahara de los Atunes** ❽, an easy-going fishing village and a popular summer escape for families from Seville. Zahara's straight, broad beach is somewhat exposed and weather-beaten, making inroads into the friendly and unpretentious town, where you will find several low-key tapas bars.

Take the A2227 via La Zarzuela to reach the N340 inland. Turn right (heading south again) and turn off right on to the CA8202 for Bolonia. Near Bolonia are the substantial Roman ruins of **Baelo Claudia** ❾ (Tue–Sat Apr–mid-June 9am–8pm, mid-June–mid-Sept 9am–3pm, mid-Sept–mid-Mar 9am–6pm, Sun year-round 9am–3pm), including the remains of an amphitheatre, paved forum and temples. Having prospered on its production of garum, a salted fish paste that was popular across the Roman Empire, the settlement is believed to have fallen into decline following an earthquake in the 2nd century.

TARIFA

Retrace your steps back to the N340 and continue south until you get to Spain's southwestern tip. A Moorish flavour pervades the town of **Tarifa** ❿, which takes its name from Tarif ibn Malik, who led a reconnaissance mission to Spain preceding the North African invasion in 711. Because of the strong Atlantic winds blowing on to the

The formidable Castillo de Guzmán

Costa de la Luz, Tarifa has built a reputation for itself as the surfing and windsurfing capital of Spain.

After dark, the streets inside its medieval walls buzz with an eclectic mix of dimly lit bars, cushion-strewn cafés, aromatic restaurants and art galleries. Laid-back and a touch bohemian, Tarifa relishes its reputation as 'a piece of washed-up Africa'. From here Tangier is a mere 35 minutes away by hydrofoil: easily doable in a day trip. FRS (www.frs.es) offers a special deal for a day in Tangier including ferry crossings, a guided tour of the Kasbah, medina and zoco, and a typical Moroccan meal.

The only sight to visit in Tarifa is the **Castillo de Guzmán** (www.castilloguzmanelbueno.com; summer daily 9.30–8.30, winter Tue–Sun 11.30am–5.30pm; guided tour at noon), originally a Moorish Alcázar, parts of which date from the 10th century. In 1292 it fell to Christian forces, but as the closest point to Africa it remained a point of conflict. Alsonso de Guzmán's heroic defence of the town two years later earned him the epithet 'El Bueno', the Good. Guzmán had sacrificed his own son rather than surrender the castle to the Muslims, and was subsequently ennobled to become the Duke of Medina Sidonia. Some 300 years later, a descendant of Guzmán led the Spanish Armada.

You might want to stay the night around Tarifa. If not, you can hop from one coast to a very different one; it's not far round the Bay of Algeciras (eastwards) to the Costa del Sol.

Food and Drink

① ALBORONÍA

Zoco de Artesanía, Plaza Peones, Jerez de la Frontera; tel: 627-992 003; tapas; €€

Although the tapas are pretty good, the main reason to come here is for its lovely location in a tree-filled courtyard. The food has a Moroccan influence and the chefs regularly come up with new ideas. Occasional live music.

⑦ PALACIO DUQUES DE MEDINA SIDONIA

Plaza Condes de Niebla, Sanlúcar de Barrameda; tel: 956-360 161; www.ruralduquesmedinasidonia.com; L and D; €

It's rare to find a good tearoom in Andalucía, so make the most of this one, which occupies a handsome 16th-century building and offers an excellent selection of cakes. It is also a hotel with nine rooms.

⑧ EL FARO DE CÁDIZ

Calle San Felix 15, Cádiz; tel: 956-225 858; www.elfarodecadiz.com; L and D; €€€

This is one of the best fish and seafood restaurants in Andalucía. If you don't want a sit-down meal, soak up the atmosphere and order hot and cold tapas from the bar. Expect prices to reflect the quality.

Dramatically sited Arcos de la Frontera

THE WHITE TOWNS

The archetypal image of Andalucía is one of a white-washed town clinging to the hillside. This easy drive links together the best of the region's famed White Towns and ends in the most dramatic of them all, the splendidly sited Ronda.

DISTANCE: 132km (82 miles)
TIME: 1 or 2 days
START: Arcos de la Frontera
END: Ronda
POINTS TO NOTE: This route can be driven in a day, but spreading it over two means you can cover each town properly. Certainly allow plenty of time for Ronda – you may want to bed down on arrival and explore it afresh the next day.

There are whitewashed towns and villages (*pueblos blancos*) all over Andalucía, but *the* White Towns cluster relatively close together in the hills of Cádiz and Málaga. As well as sharing their distinctive colour, they are almost always sited in defensive positions, as picturesque from a distance as they are close up. Typically, the White Towns are arranged around an imposing church, built as a victory statement by the Christians following the Reconquest; but it was the Moors who created these settlements – and most are still crowned by a crumbling Arab fortress. This drive

visits the most interesting of the towns, culminating in the brilliant Ronda, which should grace the list of every traveller's top sights in Andalucía.

ARCOS TO GRAZALEMA

Arcos de la Frontera ❶ is a good place to begin the route, being easily accessible from Seville by motorway. It is squeezed onto a thin limestone ridge, precariously balanced above a river valley. Easily located in the highest, oldest part of town is the **Plaza del Cabildo**. On the lip of the crag's near-vertical precipice, it benefits from far-reaching views across the River Guadalete and beyond. A luxurious **parador** hotel (see page 108) converted within the Casa del Corregidor, the 11th-century walls of the Castillo de los Duques (privately owned) and a 15th-century Gothic church, **Santa Maria de la Asunción**, flank the square.

Drive along the A372, heading due east from Arcos to **El Bosque ❷**. This refreshing town, with its tinkling fountains and an old waterwheel, is surrounded by pine trees. It slopes down

to a clear river, abundant with trout – a speciality in the local restaurants.

From this point you enter the **Parque Natural Sierra de Grazalema**, a protected area of rugged terrain, where an unusual microclimate has preserved some ancient Mediterranean forest and a precious wildlife habitat. Continue on the same road as it winds up and over the Puerto del Boyar before dropping to the town of Grazalema.

A cascade of pretty whitewashed houses snuggled into the lush foothills of the peak of San Cristóbal, **Grazalema ❸** is a welcoming, ebullient place. The town lays claim to the region's highest rainfall, and its wrought-iron balconies and geranium-filled window boxes are often coated with snow in winter. Grazalema earns its living from ceramics and woollen products, crafted according to long-established traditions, as well as tourism. You can see traditional weaving methods at the **Museo de Artesanía Textil** (http://mantasdegrazalema.com; Mon–Thu 8am–6.30pm, Fri 8am–2pm; free).

ZAHARA DE LA SIERRA TO RONDA LA VIEJA

Retrace the route a short way back along the A372 and turn right on to the CA9104, signposted for Zahara de la Sierra. Halfway to Zahara the road twists and climbs to 1,357 metres (4,452ft) at **Puerto de las Palomas**, where birds of prey (Bonnelli's, booted and golden eagles, griffon vultures and buzzards) circle watchfully, high overhead.

Zahara de la Sierra

The village of **Zahara de la Sierra ❹** wraps itself like a helter-skelter around an isolated, sheer outcrop, twisting down from the ruined 12th-century castle at its peak. An important Moorish town, it was a significant Christian conquest in 1483, and seems little changed. It is a cared-for place where a humble pride can be seen in swept steps and immaculately tended flowerbeds. The unassuming town enjoys truly majestic views across olive groves and the reservoir at the foot of its hill.

Ronda and the famous Puente Nuevo

Olvera

Follow the signs from Zahara to Algo-donales, where you meet the main road (A384) between Jerez de la Frontera and the Costa del Sol. Turn right and keep on the A384 all the way to **Olvera ❺**, one of the largest of the White Towns. Its silhouette is dramatic: a Moorish keep and the imposing Iglesia de la Encarnacíon rise above tightly packed houses sloping down to a clear perimeter where the countryside begins.

Famous as a refuge for outlaws in the 19th century, Olvera today has a reputation for excellent olive oil and religiosity. A monument to the Sacred Heart of Jesus on a natural outcrop of rock dominates the lower town, and pilgrims have been known to crawl for miles on their hands and knees, in fulfilment of a vow, to the popular sanctuary of the Virgen de los Remedios. If you have time to spare you might like to walk or cycle along the Via Verde de La Sierra (green way) that starts in Olvera. For 36km (22 miles) it follows the route of a never-used railway line to Puerto Serrano, passing through a vulture reserve on the way.

Setenil de las Bodegas

Take the CA9102 from just outside Olvera to **Setenil de las Bodegas ❻**, a small town set – not on a hilltop as is usually the case – in a ravine of the Río Guadalporcun. It has two or three streets of semi-cave houses whose roofs are formed by overhanging rock, giving their neat white facades the appearance of mushroom stems under a spreading crown. It is worth stopping for a meal or a drink at one of Setenil's characterful bars, such as **Las Flores**, see ❶.

Ronda La Vieja

Take the CA9113 before turning left on to the MA8400 to reach the ruins of **Ronda La Vieja ❼** (Old Ronda), the remains of the Roman settlement of Acinipo, which thrived between the 1st century BC and the 4th century AD. It's a beautiful place to stop for a walk. Expect great views back towards Grazalema and the mountains around it.

RONDA

Pick up the MA7402, which leads to the A374 main road. Turn left (south) and round a few curves you arrive in **Ronda ❽**.

Ronda is the best known of the White Towns and is inevitably full of tourists, thanks partly due to its location near the Costa del Sol, but also because of its own merit – it is simply the most spectacular. The town creeps up to the lip of a cliff, split in two by a plunging, deep and narrow gorge (El Tajo) carved by the River Guadalevín.

The town's impressive geography made the place a natural fortress. After the Arab invasion of 711 Ronda became one of the Moors' most important towns, known as Madinat Runda, and examples of Moorish architecture can still be seen in the old town.

Early in the 11th century, the Berber Abu Mur displaced the caliphal govern-

Casa del Rey Moro's gardens

ment, making Ronda an independent *taífa*. Later, after Christian forces had retaken Seville in 1248, the town was at the forefront of tensions between Christian Seville and Muslim Granada. But Muslim rule lasted until 1485 when, as one of the last strongholds of the Kingdom of Granada, Ronda was conquered by the Christians after a seven-day siege.

Since the 18th century when Ronda expanded outwards, the El Tajo gorge has been spanned by one of the most photographed bridges in the world, the **Puente Nuevo**, connecting the old part of town with the new. The middle part of the bridge once served as a prison.

Food and Drink

1 LAS FLORES

Avenida del Carmen 24, Setenil de las Bodegas; tel: 956-124 044; L and D; €
This busy, no-frills village bar has tables set out on a balcony with views over the gorge. The food is old fashioned and homemade; the service informal: in sum, the simplest of pleasures.

2 SIEMPRE IGUAL

Calle San José 2, Ronda; tel: 687-153 867; L and D, closed Mon; €
This bar, near the bus station, complements its food with a great selection of local wines. For more on Ronda's wines, see www.ruta-vinos-ronda.com.

Ronda's new town

After exploring the bridge, make for the **bullring** (daily Apr–Sept 10am–8pm, Oct and Mar 10am–7pm, Jan–Feb and Nov–Dec 10am–6pm; closed on bull-fighting days) in the 'new' town. It is the oldest in Spain and has a bullfighting museum (same hours) inside. Modern bullfighting – on foot rather than mounted on horseback – is thought to have originated in Ronda in the 18th century. In commemoration, a bullfight in period dress, the Corrida Goyesca, is held during the town's fair in September. Nearby **Siempre Igual** – see 2 – will satisfy empty bellies.

Ronda's old town

All the other sights are across the bridge in the old (Moorish) town, sometimes referred to as La Ciudad. Worth seeking out are the **Iglesia Santa María de la Mayor** (built over a mosque in the 13th century, its bell tower fashioned out of the minaret); **Palacio del Mondragón**, now the town's museum (with a handsome Renaissance facade); **Casa del Gigante** (surviving from the Muslim era); the **Casa del Rey Moro**, with its hanging gardens; and the **Baños Arabes** (Arab baths).

Note that if you want to take in the standard photographed view of Puente Nuevo, you will need to follow the path down from Plaza del Campillo (at the end of Calle Tenorio). Alternatively, you can drive down Camino de los Molinos (from the Puerta de Almocabar) and climb up to the Arco Arabe.

Plaza del Socorro, Ronda   Gibraltar town centre

GIBRALTAR

Officially British, but geographically joined to the Costa del Sol, Gibraltar is a delightful anomaly that makes a great day out. Its highpoint is the great Rock, a nature reserve inhabited by semi–wild monkeys, with stupendous views from the top.

DISTANCE: 7km (4.5 miles)
TIME: 1 day
START & END: Casemates Square
POINTS TO NOTE: Traffic can be heavy; most people make use of the private car parks in La Línea and then either walk to Casemates Square or take a bus (No. 5 or 10). Holders of UK, Australian, Irish, New Zealand and US passports do not need a visa to enter Gibraltar. All other nationals should check www.gibraltarborder.gi/visa. The local currency is the Gibraltarian pound, but shops accept euros.

Gibraltar inhabits one of the world's most strategic locations, looking across the narrow straits to the nearby North African coast. The rock has served as a maritime landmark since ancient times, but the first settlement wasn't constructed until after the Moors invaded in 711. Gibraltar was reconquered by Spanish Christian forces in 1462, but lost to the British through the 1713 Treaty of Utrecht. In 1779–83 Spanish and French forces besieged Gibraltar, but the outpost did not surrender. Spain still nominally claims sovereignty of this British Crown Colony, but most Gibraltarians are happy with their status. Gibraltar is culturally British, with many cosmopolitan influences in the mix.

You'll want to spend the best part of the day exploring the Upper Rock, but it's worth seeing some of the town before you make the ascent.

TOWN CENTRE

The fulcrum of Gibraltar is **Casemates Square ❶**, named after the military barracks that runs along the north side. Now a lively social hub, the square was once the site of public executions.

Take pedestrianised **Main Street**, cutting through the middle of the town. It is lined with duty-free shops selling alcohol, perfume and electronic goods, and English-style pubs serving pints of bitter.

On the way you pass the top of John Macintosh Square (on which stands the **tourist information office** and **Gibraltar National Art Gallery**), then the **Cathedral of St Mary the Crowned**

The Rock

and **Gibraltar Museum** (www.gib museum.gi; Mon–Fri 10am–6pm, Sat 10am–2pm), which includes what are considered to be the best-preserved Moorish baths in Europe. Afterwards come the **Supreme Court** and **The Convent**, a former monastery now housing the **Governor's Residence**. If you are lucky you'll catch the ceremonial changing of the guard (Mon–Thu 11am–4pm, Fri 11am–1pm).

UPPER ROCK

Main Street ends at the **Referendum Gates**. Fork left up Referendum Roads to the **cable-car departure station ❷** (every 15 minutes daily summer 9.30am–7.15pm, winter until 5.15pm), located next to **Alameda Botanic Gardens** (8am–sunset; free).

The views from the **top station ❸** on the 412 metres (1,352ft) summit are truly spectacular. Refuel in the **Top of the Rock Café ❶**.

You are now in the **Upper Rock Nature Reserve** (daily 9am–6.15pm, later in summer), which has dense Mediterranean scrub vegetation harbouring 530 kinds of plant, including some rare species, growing on the alkaline limestone soils. This area is good for birdwatching too, especially during the spring and summer migrations when Gibraltar marks the shortest route between Europe and Africa.

From the top station walk south along St Michael's Road to reach **St Michael's Cave ❹** (same opening times as nature reserve), an impressive natural grotto containing stalagmites and stalactites, which is sometimes used as a venue

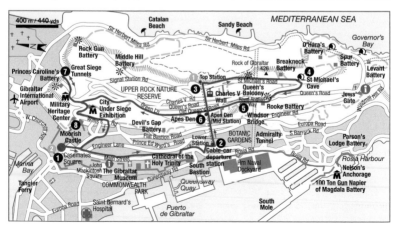

St Michael's Cave

for musical performances. The cave is so deep that it was once thought to connect to North Africa.

Head north along Queen's road to Queen's Balcony, another worthy viewpoint. Retrace your steps slightly to take the Royal Anglian Way footpath and **Windsor Bridge ❺**, spanning a 50-metre/yd wide gorge. If you don't have a head for heights, skip the bridge by continuing along Queen's Road from the Balcony.

Either way, you'll meet Old Queen's Road, leading to the **Apes' Den ❻**. The so-called Barbary apes (actually tailless macaque monkeys) that inhabit the Rock are natives of North Africa, descended from animals brought over by sailors as pets and ships' mascots in the 18th century. Legend has it that if the apes ever leave the Rock, British rule will end. Be aware that the apes can be mischievous; they've been known to snatch handbags and cameras, and can react aggressively if they feel threatened. Keep calm and maintain a discreet distance.

Keep along Old Queen's Road to the extreme north end of the rock, where a right fork at Princess Caroline's Battery takes you to the **Great Siege Tunnels ❼** (same opening times as nature reserve), a system of galleries blasted through the inside of the rock face during the 18th-century. Note that the cannon emplacements slope downwards, a clever innovation that allowed the defenders to fire directly at the Spanish and French forces attacking from La Línea.

In total, the Rock conceals around 50km (31 miles) of military tunnels, but not all are open to the public. The left fork from Princess Caroline's Battery takes you to some excavated for use during World War II (visitable by reservation, tel: +350-2007 1649).

Nearby is the **Moorish Castle ❽** (same opening times as nature reserve), the remains of a once massive fortress dating partly from the 14th century.

Descend Willis's Road and half way down take the flight of steps on the right (Castle Steps). Turn right on to another flight of steps (Castle Ramp), leading to the back of Casemates Square. Go down Crutchett's Ramp and into the square to finish the walk. There are several places to eat and drink – make for **The Lord Nelson ❷** to take the weight off your feet.

Food and Drink

❶ TOP OF THE ROCK CAFÉ
Cable Car Top Station; tel: +350-2007 8759; L; €
Self-service cafeteria with unbeatable views, selling snacks, light meals and hot and cold drinks.

❷ THE LORD NELSON
Unit 10 Casemates Square; www.lordnelson. gi; tel: +350-2005 0009; B, L and D; €
This themed pub is a good place to order British classics: think fish and chips and burgers.

Relaxing in the Plaza de los Naranjos

MARBELLA OLD TOWN

It's easy to visit bustling and sophisticated Marbella and not realise there is an exquisite old quarter set back from the beach and the shops. This short route is a delightful stroll around its picturesque streets and squares.

DISTANCE: 2km (1.25 miles)
TIME: 2 hours
START: Avenida Ramón y Cajal
END: Marbella seafront

Marbella has become world famous as a tourist resort, but it started life as a small, whitewashed coastal village.

HEART OF THE OLD TOWN

Begin by walking up Calle Huerta Chica from Marbella's central spine – the **Avenida Ramón y Cajal ❶** – into the old town. The street kinks right and becomes pedestrianised in front of **La Pesquera**, see ❶, leading into Plaza de la Victoria.

Museo del Bonsai

Just north of the route in the Parque Arroyo de la Represa, the Museo del Bonsai (tel: 952-862 926) has an excellent collection of dwarf wild olive trees.

Plaza de los Naranjos
Continue across the square on Calle de la Estación to reach the **Plaza de los Naranjos ❷**, the heart of the old town and of Marbella itself, named after the orange trees that grace its centre. The square was laid out in the 16th century, with a deliberate regularity that contrasts the erratic Moorish alleys around it. Bar and restaurant tables line the plaza; soak up the atmosphere from the **Casa del Corregidor ❷**, situated in the historic Chief Magistrate's House (1552). The building has a Gothic-Mudejar stone portico, an attractive iron balcony and a Renaissance gallery above.

The main building overlooking the square, however, is the **Ayuntamiento** (town hall), with the tourist information office occupying one corner of it. In the plaza's southwest corner is Marbella's first church, the 15th-century **Ermita de Santiago**. It sits at an angle to the square; its odd orientation suggests it was built before the rest of the square was conceived.

Iglesia de Nuestra Señora de la Encarnación

Main church and the Museo del Grabado Contemporaneo

Take the street opposite the Casa del Corregidor, Calle General Chincilla, which brings you to a sloping whitewashed wall. Above this looms Marbella's old Arab wall, the earliest parts dating from the 9th century. Turn right along Calle Carmen into the square beside Marbella's main church, the 17th-century **Iglesia de Nuestra Señora de la Encarnación ❸**. Turn immediately left (following the city wall – the lowest stones here are thought to be of Roman origin) along the dog-legged Calle Trinidad.

At the next crossroads turn right down Calle Salinas and take the first left to the **Museo del Grabado Contemporaneo ❹** (Museum of Contemporary Engraving; www.mgec.es; Mon and Sat 9am–2pm, Tue–Fri 9am–7pm). The museum inhabits a Renaissance building, the Hospital de Bazán, which has a handsome gallery on its uppermost floor; the collection inside includes works by Miró and Picasso.

Plazas Castillo and Santo Cristo

Retrace your steps to the end of Calle Trinidad and carry straight on up Calle Salinas, with the city walls on your left. You emerge briefly on Calle Arte, stepping for a moment outside the old town. Take the flight of steps to your left, passing a shrine in a rock overhang, and enter **Plaza Castillo ❺**. There is only one way out of this, into the adjacent Plaza de San Bernabé. Continue straight across this square and descend the broad flight of steps into

Puerto Banús

Calle Carmen (the street which you came along earlier). Turn right up Calle Ortiz de Molinillos, which swings left, beneath a statue of the Virgin Mary set into the wall, to become Calle Remedios.

This brings you to Plaza Puente de Ronda, the site of one of the city's old gateways. Turn right up Calle Ancha, the main street of the Barrio Alto, a 'new town' laid out in straight streets beyond the city walls after the conquest of Marbella in 1485. Handsome houses line Calle Ancha; note also the lanes off to the right, filled with colourful plant pots. Continue as far as the pretty **Plaza del Santo Cristo** ❻, named for its church, which boasts a distinctive blue and white chequered spire. If you want an Andalucían finale to your evening, return here for the show at Flamenco Ana Maria (see page 120).

Double back down Calle Ancha and turn right down Calle Princesa. At the end, make a left down Calle Aduar, bring-ing you back to the Plaza Puente de Ronda. Take Pasaje Cruz to return to the Plaza de los Naranjos – cross the square and leave it by the street next to the chapel, Pasaje Valdés. Turn right at the bottom and left out of the Plaza Africa on Calle Africa to leave the old town.

LEAVING THE OLD TOWN

Straight ahead, across Avenida Ramón y Cajal, is **Parque de la Alameda** ❼ with its striking middle fountain, a park characterised by its attractive, crumbling ceramic benches. Walk through the park, following **Avenida del Mar** ❽, lined with statues cast from moulds made by Salvador Dali, to end at Marbella's seafront.

Puerto Banús

The slick suburb of Nueva Andalucía is a world away from the old quarter with its famous jet-setter's harbor, Puerto Banús. Unbelievably expensive yachts line the quayside; Porsches, Rolls-Royces and Ferraris fill the streets; and a glamorous line-up of exclusive restaurants and high-class boutiques seem permanently open. Even if you can't afford to join in, it's fun to watch how the other half lives – you might just spot a celebrity.

Food and Drink

❶ LA PESQUERA

Plaza de la Victoria; tel: 952-765 170; http://lapesquera.com; L and D; €€
One of a chain of seafood restaurants, popular with the locals, where you can choose your meal from the fish tank.

❷ CASA DEL CORREGIDOR

Plaza de los Naranjos 6; tel: 651-216 992; www.casadelcorregidor.es; L and D; €€
Situated in a 16th-century magistrate's house in the main square of old Marbella, this family-run restaurant specialises in fish and seafood. Reservations are required at the weekend.

Málaga and the Catedral

MÁLAGA CITY

The capital of the Costa del Sol is at once a beach resort, port, shopping centre – and a city of history and art. This route spends a leisurely day exploring its best sights, ranging from Roman remains to the works of Pablo Picasso.

DISTANCE: 4km (2.5 miles)
TIME: 1 day
START: Catedral
END: Plaza de la Constitución
POINTS TO NOTE: The route visits four great art museums; how much time you spend in each will vary according to personal taste.

The international airport in Málaga is the main gateway to the Costa del Sol, but few people spend much time in the city itself. This is a shame, because Málaga is an ancient Andalucían city of considerable charm, and – despite being a shopping and service centre – hasn't lost its heart to commercialism.

Originally Phoenician, Málaga sided briefly with Carthage before becoming a Roman *municipium* (a town governed by its own laws). In 711 it fell to the Moors. In recent decades, its magnificent collection of historical remains has been joined by a cluster of world-class art museums. Málaga also benefits from great shops, superb bars and restaurants and a thriving nightlife scene.

THE CATEDRAL AND MUSEO PICASSO

The best way to begin a tour of Málaga is at the city's most prominent landmark, the **Catedral** ❶ (www.diocesisMálaga. es/catedral; Apr–mid-Oct Mon–Fri 10am–9pm, Sat 10am–6.30pm, Sun 2–6.30pm, mid-Oct–Mar Mon–Fri 10am–6.30pm, Sat 10am–5.30pm, Sun 2–5.30pm). Built in fits and starts between 1528 and 1782, it is still unfinished, as one of its twin towers is missing – the other rises an impressive 100 metres (328ft) above street level. From that, it gets its nickname, 'La Manquita', the One-Armed Lady. The highlight of the interior is the choir, completed in 1662 by the great Granada sculptor Pedro de Mena. On the square in front of the cathedral's western facade is the **Palacio Episcopal** (Bishop's Palace), a venue for temporary art exhibitions.

A short walk north from the cathedral, on Calle San Augustín, is the magnifi-

The pretty courtyard of the Museo Picasso

cent Buenavista Palace, built between 1516 and 1542 by Diego de Cazalla and housing the **Museo Picasso** ❷ (www.museopicassoMálaga.org; daily Mar–June and Sept–Oct 10am–7pm, July–Aug 10am–8pm, Nov–Feb 10am–6pm), dedicated to Málaga's most famous son. Comprising 233 paintings, drawings, sculptures, ceramics and prints, spanning Picasso's entire career, the bulk of the collection was donated by Cristina and Bernard Ruiz-Picasso, Picasso's daughter-in-law and grandson. Works of art on display range from a portrait of his younger sister Lola, painted when he was just 15, to familiar Cubist works painted from 1910 onwards.

THE FORTIFICATIONS

Retrace your steps down Calle San Augustín and turn left along Calle Cister to reach Málaga's archaeological monuments, bunched together on the high ground at the east end of the city centre. Enter the site from Plaza de la Aduana. The route up passes through a maze of pretty gardens to the **Arco del Cristo** (Gateway of Christ) – where the Catholic Monarchs celebrated Mass following their conquest of the fortress in 1487 – and then to an old palace housing an archaeological museum.

At the foot of the route is the **Teatro Romano** ❸ (Roman Theatre; Tue–Sat 10am–6pm, Sun 10am–4pm; free). Dominating everything, however, is the **Alcazaba** ❹ (daily 9am–6pm, until 8pm in summer), and the **Castillo de Gibralfaro** ❺ (same hours as Alcazaba) above it. Connecting the two, a formidable set of double walls with square turrets ascends the hill.

The Castillo is named from the Arabic Jebel al Faro (Lighthouse Hill); this immense structure was founded by Abd-al-Rahman I in the 8th century and enlarged in the 14th century. A rocky path climbs beside the wall to a height of 130 metres (425ft), though tired legs may want to make use of the bus (No. 35). A *mirador* offers superb views over the harbour and down to the Plaza de Toros. You may want to step into the parador hotel for a drink.

ALONG THE WATERFRONT

Returning from the Alcazaba hill to the Plaza de la Aduana, turn left towards the seafront. Cross the Paseo del Parque and behind the Muelle Uno shopping

Casa Natal Picasso

If you are really keen on Picasso you may want to make a detour to visit the family home on Plaza de la Merced, near to the Museo Picasso, where he spent the first 10 years of his life. It has been restored, and functions as the Casa Natal (www.fundacionpicasso.Málaga.eu; daily 9.30am–8pm), primarily a study centre and reference library, but with a collection of family photographs, sketches and pots.

Plaza de la Merced, where Pablo Picasso was born

mall you will find the **Centre Pompidou Málaga** ❻ (Pasaje Doctor Carillo Casaux; www.centrepompidou-Málaga. eu; Wed–Mon 9.30am–8pm). This branch of the Paris institution is housed in a striking, long, low building topped by a glass 'Rubik's Cube'. It houses a stunning collection of contemporary art.

The nearby seafront area known as **La Malagueta** has many restaurants and bars serving good fish and seafood.

From Muelle Uno, follow the waterfront westwards to reach the Muelle de Heredia and a 70-metre (230ft) tall big wheel, the **Noria Mirador Princess** ❼ (http://noriamiradorprincess.com; daily

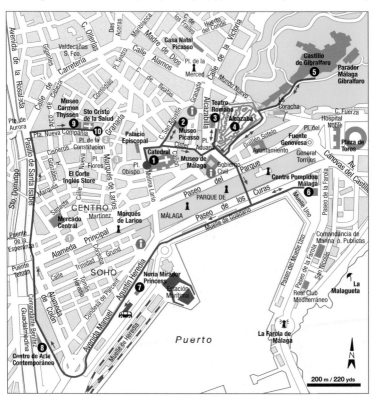

10.30am–9.30pm). It may seem somewhat out of place, but is still a novel way to get a view of the city.

The triangle of streets north of here, between Avenida Manuel Agustin Heredia and Alameda Principal, known as **Soho**, have been decorated with street art and are crammed with hip cafés, bars and boutiques. On the Alameda itself is a venerable old bar worth dipping into, the **Antigua Casa de Guardia**, see ❶.

Continue along the waterfront from the big wheel. Just beyond the Alameda de Colón, turn right up Calle Alemania to visit the **Centro de Arte Contemporáneo** ❽ (www.cacMálaga.eu; Tue–Sun June–Aug 10am–2pm and 5–9pm, Sept–May 10am–8pm; free), another superb art gallery, displaying works by leading national and international artists.

THE THYSSEN MUSEUM

Now follow the dry bed of the River Guadalmedina, which separates the city centre from the western suburbs, passing Puente Tetuan (at the end of Alameda Principal) and Puente de la Esperanza to continue up Pasillo de Santa Isabel until you come to Puerta Nueva. Turn right down Calle Compania to reach yet another renowned gallery, the **Museo Carmen Thyssen** ❾ (Calle Compañia; www.carmenthyssen-Málaga.org; Tue–Sun 10am–8pm), housed in a renovated 16th-century palace. This gallery maintains a focus on 19th-century Spanish and Andalucían art. From the museum it's short step into the **Plaza de la Constitución** ❿; stop at **Café Central** ❷, where they make a big show of getting your coffee just right. If you need something more substantial, continue a short way to **El Chinitas** ❸ for a full meal or a selection of tapas.

Food and Drink

❶ ANTIGUA CASA DE GUARDIA

Alameda Principal, 18; tel: 952-214 680; www.antiguacasadeguardia.com; €€
A Málaga institution since 1840. There are no tables or chairs, but a long wooden bar upon which the tab is chalked up. Huge old barrels hold a selection of Málaga wines.

❷ CAFÉ CENTRAL

Plaza de la Constitución 11; tel: 952-224 972; www.cafecentralMálaga.com; B, L and tapas; €
On the wall are semi-serious 'instructions for how to order a coffee in Málaga': whether you like it long, strong, short, with lots of milk or with hardly any, there is a name for your preference. The café is also a restaurant, one of its specialities being anchovies.

❸ EL CHINITAS

Calle Moreno Monroy, 4; tel: 952-210 972; www.elchinitas.com; L and D; €€€
Traditional-style Andalucían restaurant with attached tapas bar, just off the Pasaje de Chinitas in the old part of city.

CAMINITO DEL REY

The Caminito del Rey (King's Little Pathway) is a spectacular aerial walkway running high along the sides of two consecutive gorges. It makes an exhilarating family day out: an opportunity to get some fresh air, exercise and have lots of fun at the same time.

DISTANCE: 6.5–8km (4–5 miles), depending on where you park
TIME: Half a day
START: The north gate
END: El Chorro village
POINTS TO NOTE: Numbers are limited and reservation online (http://reservas.caminitodelrey.info; tel: 902-787 325) is essential. The walk is open daily Tue–Sun, but avoid the middle of the day in summer when it can be fiercely hot. If you're arriving by train (El Chorro station), a shuttle bus will take you to the start of the walk. If you're arriving by road, park in the car park beside the Embalse Conde de Guadalhorce reservoir and take the pedestrian tunnel, about 1.5km (1 mile) from the start. A new visitor centre is about to open with a large car park, but this is some distance from the footpath itself.

The route is one way only, north to south. It is perfectly safe, but you'll need a head for heights, especially to get across the suspension bridge near the end. Supervisors walk along the route offering assistance if needed; if you prefer, you can join a guided tour.

North of the town of Alora, the Guadalhorce River squeezes through a narrow gorge that separates two reservoirs forming part of Málaga's so-called 'Lake District'. In 1921 King Alfonso XIII came to inaugurate one of the dams and to impress him a catwalk of concrete and iron was built along the high walls of the gorge. The original parapet gradually fell into ruin, to be reopened in 2015 in accordance with modern safety standards. The walk proper begins at the north gate but getting there takes some planning.

DESFILADERO DE GAITANEJOS

At the **north gate ❶**, beside the **Embalse de Gaintanejo**, you'll be given a helmet and safety instructions. Buy plenty of water and take advantage of the toilets – there are no more until the end of the route. Walkers are carefully spaced out (for safety reasons), so you may have to wait a little before setting off.

The first part of the route is through a gorge, the **Desfiladero de Gaitanejos** ❷, which is impressive enough but not nearly as dramatic as what's to come. Here and there you can see stretches of the original parapet walkway that have fallen into ruin.

After approximately 900 metres (0.5 miles) you leave the gorge behind and the walking becomes much gentler as you cross the **Valle de Hoyo** ❸, a stretch of pine wood and scrubland. From here you can avoid the next stretch of vertiginous parapet by taking a 300-metre/yd **tunnel** ❹; this can prove useful in inclement weather but you do bypass a rather spectacular stretch.

DESFILADERO DE LOS GAITANES

The second canyon, **Desfiladero de los Gaitanes** ❺, is truly arresting, and boasts an overhanging glass-floored platform that may take some nerve to walk on. Round a few more corners is the climax of the walk, the **Puente Colgante** ❻, a steel suspension bridge. It's only short, but it sways slightly and the lattice floor means you can see straight down to the water below. If you don't like heights, look straight ahead and walk slowly and calmly until you get to the other side.

On the other side, the footpath descends in steps and crosses over the railway line to reach the south gate. From here a track leads above the reservoir of **Embalse de Tajo de la Encantada** to the village of **El Chorro** ❼, where you return your helmet. There's a snack kiosk and bar, **Bar Estación**, see ❶, beside the railway station. If you've come by car, a half-hourly service will collect you from the station and deposit you at the start of the walk.

Food and Drink

❶ BAR ESTACIÓN
El Chorro railway station; €
Just the place for a cold drink and a snack after walking the caminito, while waiting for your bus or train.

Priego de Córdoba

GRANADA TO CÓRDOBA
THE SLOW WAY

The middle of Andalucía is often overlooked by tourists, but those who venture inland are rewarded with beautiful landscapes and pretty historic towns. This route cherry-picks the most interesting places to stop on the back roads between Granada and Córdoba.

DISTANCE: 249km (155 miles)
TIME: 2 days
START: Granada
END: Córdoba
POINTS TO NOTE: Priego de Córdoba and Zuheros have good overnight options to break the route – see page 109.

The N432 provides a quick link between Granada and Córdoba, the two great Islamic cities of Andalucía, for those in a hurry. If time is on your side, however, this is the way to go – this slow but scenic route makes use of country roads to visit several picturesque towns and villages along the way.

GRANADA TO ALCALÁ LA REAL

Leave **Granada ❶** heading west on the A92 through Santa Fé. Turn off onto the A336 heading north to reach **Montefrio ❷**, a hill town underneath an old castle, its streets gathered around a circular, domed church.

Continue north out of Montefrio on the N335. At Los Agramaderos you enter Jaen province. Across the other side of the N432 (the road you are deliberately not taking) is **Alcalá la Real ❸**. This was a fortified Moorish city from the early 8th century and remained a strategic bastion until the Reconquest of Granada in 1492, after which further Christian monuments were added. The **Fortaleza de la Mota** (daily Apr–Sept 10.30am–7.30pm, Oct–Mar 10am–5.30pm), on the summit of a hill, is an amazing complex combining Moorish and Christian influences, with fabulous, stretching views. Inside it is the abbey church of Santa María la Mayor, built on the site of the former mosque.

You will need to head back down to the shopping and business part of town if you're in need of refreshments. **Restaurante Torrepalma ❶** may not look all that inviting from the outside, but its tapas are exceedingly good.

PRIEGO DE CÓRDOBA

Take the N339 from Alcalá due west into Córdoba province to reach **Priego de Córdoba ❹**, the jewel of the prov-

Zuheros's castle

ince. It is situated on a bluff above the Río Salado, a salt-water river.

Known as the capital of 18th-century Andalucían Baroque architecture, Priego has several beautiful churches in this style, notably the **Parroquia de la Asunción** (Tue–Sat 11am–1.30pm, Sun 11–11.30am and 1–1.30pm), with a white-and-gold dome in the Sagrario chapel. The **Fuente del Rey** is a monumental Baroque fountain with 139 spouts. Locals say that when the water level is high enough to cover the private parts of Neptune's statue, there will be sufficient water for the crops.

During the 18th century, Priego's thriving silk industry brought prosperity to the town. The fine buildings, including a number of noble mansions with handsome wrought-iron balconies and window grilles, date from that time. The old quarter of town, where passageways are no more than an arm's breadth, dates from Moorish times. Here, neighbours keep up the curious custom of carrying an image of a favourite saint, complete with tiny altar in a carry-case, from house to house. A complex schedule allows each family to keep it for one day.

There are plenty of bars and restaurants to choose from in Priego. One good, inexpensive place is **Califato**, see ②.

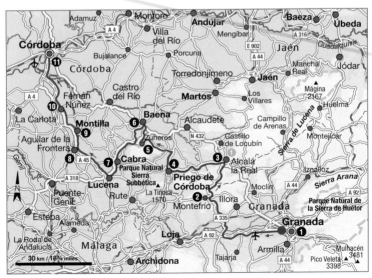

Cueva de los Murciélagos

Baena

ZUHEROS

Head north from Priego on the A333 as far as Fuente Alhama, where you turn left on the CO8209, heading through Morellana to reach Luque, built against a grey rock. At the roundabout, pick up the CO6207 to **Zuheros** ❺, with its Moorish castle, Museo Arqueológico (Tue–Fri 10am–2pm and 5–7pm in summer, 4–6pm in winter, Sat–Sun hours vary; admission charge includes visit to the castle) and maze of narrow streets. High above the village is the **Cueva de los Murciélagos** (Cave of Bats), which has interesting rock formations and Neolithic art. It is visited by guided tour (tel: 957-694 545; http://turismodelasubbetica.es/zuheros; Apr–Sept Tue–Fri at 12.30pm and 3.30pm, Sat–Sun 11am, 12.30pm, 2pm, 5pm and 6.30pm, Oct–Mar Tue–Fri 12.30pm and 4.30pm, Sat–Sun 11am, 12.30pm, 2pm, 4pm and 5.30pm). The ticket office is in the Ecomuseo (Ecomuseum) in the car park some way from the entrance to the cave. Finds from the cave are on display in the Archaeology Museum.

Take the road due north out of Zuheros (CO6209). Cross the main road and continue north on the A3128.

BAENA AND CABRA

Follow the signs into **Baena** ❻. The prosperous Muslim town of Bayyana developed on this site thanks to rich soils and plentiful water. Olive oil produced in Baena, under a Denominación de Origen, is said to be among the best in Spain. At the top of the hill, you will find the historical part of town, La Almedina, including the remains of a Moorish fortress castle. The Gothic church of Santa María has an Isabelline portal. Beside the church is the 16th-century Convent of Madre de Dios, with an unusual balcony, the Arco de la Villa, arching over the street. On the edge of the old town are two Moorish gateways.

Take the CO6202 south to **Doña Mencía** and continue on the CO6201 to reach **Cabra** ❼. The narrow streets behind the church of La Asuncion y Angeles are lined with whitewashed houses. Another church, San Juan Bautista, is one of the oldest in Andalucía, having been founded in the 7th century.

Shepherd taking a break, Zuheros

Bodegas Espejo, Montilla

AGUILAR TO CÓRDOBA

Take the A342 due west to meet the N331, which leads to **Aguilar de la Frontera ❽**, formed around an octagonal main square. Five kilometres (3 miles) out of town is the **Laguna de Zónar**, a nature reserve which attracts waterfowl in winter, including the rare white-headed duck (with a conspicuous blue bill).

From Aguilar it is a short drive up the N331 to reach the turning for **Montilla ❾**, where wine has been made since the 8th century BC. Comparisons with sherry are inevitable, for Montilla wines are produced by the *solera* system of blending in the same way as the more widely marketed Jerez wines. These days a light, young white wine, rather similar to the Vinho Verde from northern Portugal, is being produced around here.

The bodegas (wineries) will be happy to show you around and give you samples to taste. The oldest winery is **Bodegas Alvear** in Montilla (tel: 957-652 939; www.alvear.es; tours Mon–Sat at 12.30pm; reservation required). Other wineries offering guided tours include Bodegas Cruz Conde (tel: 957-651 250; www.bodegascruzconde.es; Mon–Sat at noon) and Pérez Barquero (tel: 957-650 500; www.perezbarquero.com; visits on request). The region celebrates its wine festival in the last week of August.

Follow the signs for Córdoba out of Montilla and you'll find yourself back on the N331. The road goes through Montemayor, which has a ruined castle, and then **Fernán Núñez ❿**, dominated by its restored 18th-century ducal palace.

Complete the route by taking the A45 motorway into the city of **Córdoba ⓫**, which you can explore on route 12 in the morning, should you wish.

Food and Drink

❶ RESTAURANTE TORREPALMA

Calle Conde de Torrepalma, Alcalá la Real; tel: 953-583 010; www.restaurantetorrepalma.com; L and D; €
You'll find this place in the commercial part of town: it's just right if you're looking for something functional rather than fussy. In addition to hearty main dishes it puts on an excellent selection of tapas, *raciones*, sandwiches, toasted sandwiches and *platos combinados* such as ham, egg and chips.

❷ CALIFATO

Calle Abad palomino, Priego de Córdoba; tel: 957-543 233; B, L and D; €
Califato commands a good atmosphere, whether you eat indoors or out, and staff are helpful. Its speciality dish is *flammenquin*: thin slices of pork rolled up with mountain-cured ham and deep fried. If you're here in winter, pick a table inside near the fire.

Moorish influence is obvious in the Plaza del Triunfo

CÓRDOBA

Córdoba is a labyrinth of winding alleyways and Moorish patios, spread around a bend in the River Guadalquivir. Its supreme monument is La Mezquita, a vast 10th-century mosque of harmonious pillars and arches.

DISTANCE: 2.5km (1.5 miles)
TIME: Half a day
START: Plaza del Triunfo
END: Mezquita (Mosque)
POINTS TO NOTE: Córdoba is easy to visit on a day-trip from Seville, either by car or on the high-speed AVE train. However, to avoid feeling rushed, we recommend spending the night.

Most visitors come to Córdoba to see just one building, the extraordinary Mezquita (Mosque) that forms the highlight of this walking tour; and you should certainly allow time to do this grand monument justice. But don't let that blind you to Córdoba's other attractions, many of which are contained within a compact area near the mosque, particularly in the old Jewish quarter of the city.

Córdoba is one of the oldest cities in Spain. In 206 BC it was invaded by the Romans, who later made it the capital of the Roman province of Further Spain. In 572, after nearly eight centuries of Roman rule, the Visigoths took control of the city. In 711 it fell to the Moors, and in 756 Abd-al-Rahman I, Amir of the Umayyad dynasty, established it as an independent emirate ruling most of the Iberian Peninsula.

Abd-al-Rahman III raised the city to the status of Caliphate in 929 and ushered in a golden age. Considered to be one of the cultural capitals of the world, second in wealth and culture only to Constantinople, the city was a respected centre of science and art. It had the first street lighting in Europe and a library containing over 400,000 volumes. Estimates of the population at that time range from 500,000 to one million.

This prosperity came to an abrupt end with the rebellion of Muhammad II al-Mahdi in 1009, a development that led to the disintegration of the Caliphate and triggered a long decline in the city's fortunes. By the time Córdoba was reconquered in 1236 by Fernando III, the city was in ruins. In 1382 Alfonso XI ordered the construction of the *alcázar*, which became the residence of Queen Isabel towards the end of the 15th century.

The illuminated Puente Romano

THE RIVER

Begin the walk in the **Plaza del Triunfo ❶**, the riverside square across the road from the Mezquita. Here you'll find the tourist office, an 18th-century statue of the archangel St Raphael, patron of the city, and a ceremonial gateway, the Puerta del Puente, which houses a small museum and has a viewing platform at the top.

Take a few steps on to the Roman Bridge, the **Puente Romano ❷**, a good place to come back to at sunset for views over the old town. In the river bottom, overgrown with rushes where ducks paddle, are the remains of three Arabic watermills, the **Molinos Arabes**.

On the far side of the bridge is the **Torre de la Calahorra ❸** (www.torrecalahorra. es; daily May–Sept 10am–2pm and 4.30–8.30pm, Oct–Apr 10am–6pm), a 14th-century watchtower that houses a museum depicting the glories of al-Andalus (Muslim Spain).

THE ALCÁZAR AND ITS BATHS

From the Plaza del Triunfo, follow the riverbank downstream (southwest) beside the seminary and you will come to the corner of the **Alcázar de los Reyes Cristianos ❹** (Tue–Sun 8.30am–8.15pm, Sat 8.30am–4pm, Sun 8.30am–2pm), a palace built by Alfonso XI in the 14th century on the site of previous Visigoth and Moorish fortresses. For many years it was the home of the Catholic Monarchs, who received Columbus and planned the Reconquest of Granada here. Following the fall of Granada in 1492, the palace was used by the Court of Inquisition, and then functioned as a civil jail and military prison.

Inside, the highlight of the palace is the **Hall of the Mosaics**, featuring Roman mosaics and a Roman stone sarcophagus dating from the 2nd or 3rd century AD. Outside, four towers guard the walls, with the tops of those open to visitors providing an excellent platform to view (and take photographs of) La Mezquita. The extensive gardens are a peaceful place, the design of which includes a series of rectangular ponds similar to, but not as stunning as, those at the Generalife in Granada (see page 93).

Behind are the **Caballeria Reales ❺** (Royal Stables; www.caballerizasreales. com), which can also be visited.

Across the road from the Alcázar is Plaza Campo Santo de los Martires and the **Baños del Alcázar Califal ❻** (http://banosdelalcazarcalifal.cordoba. es; same hours as Alcázar), the palace's ornately decorated 10th-century baths. The **Almudaina**, see ❶, is a good (if pricey) place to eat on this square.

INTO THE JUDERÍA

Go up Calle Tomás Conde and fork left beside the hotel Casas de la Judería; you soon reach **La Judería** itself, Córdoba's medieval Jewish quarter. If Córdoba is known for the splendour of its 10th-

Gardens of the Alcázar   Decorated houses, La Judería

century achievements in art, architecture and science, a part of its glory is attributed to the Sephardim community, the Spanish Jews who settled here during the time of the Roman emperors, when they were allowed the same rights as other inhabitants of Baetica, Roman Spain.

Under the Visigoths Jews were persecuted so severely that they welcomed the Muslim invaders. In exchange, they enjoyed long periods of peaceful coexistence, and a flowering of Sephardim culture during which many achieved rare heights in diplomacy, medicine, commerce and crafts.

You soon come to Plaza Maimónides, dominated by a Baroque mansion that has been turned into the **Museo Taurino** ❼ (Mon–Fri 8.30am–8.15pm, Sun 8.30am–2.30pm), one of the most comprehensive bullfighting museums in Spain. Exhibits include bulls' heads, suits of light (trajes de luces), posters and a display on the life of the famous local torero Manolete, who was killed by a bull in Linares in 1947. Adjacent to the museum is the richly decorated Chapel of San Bartolomé.

Calle Judíos

Take Calle Judíos. Stop on the left in **Plaza Tiberiades** to admire the statue of Maimonides, one of the greatest philosophers in Jewish history. A rabbi and Talmudic scholar with an Aristotelian bent, Maimonides was born in Córdoba in 1135. His family fled to Morocco to escape repression and he eventually settled in Egypt, but Córdoba still claims him as a native son.

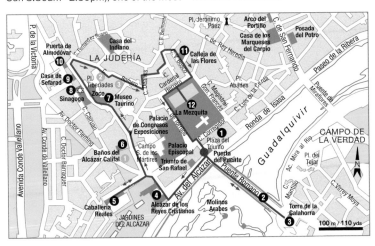

La Mezquita in all its glory

Further on, on the same side of the street, is the **Sinagoga** ❽ (currently closed), built in 1315 and one of only three medieval synagogues remaining in Spain. Segments of Hebraic inscriptions and family history remain on the walls. The upper gallery, where women were seated, and the niche where the Torah was kept, are still intact.

Next you come to the **Casa de Sefarad** ❾ (www.casadesefarad.es; daily 10am–7pm), a fascinating museum focusing on the life of Spanish Jews, and the **Casa Andalusí** (No 12; lacasaandalusi.es; daily 10am–7pm), a pretty 12th-century house with Islamic decoration.

At the top of Calle Judíos is the **Zoco Municipal** (daily 10am–8pm; free), a cluster of craft workshops huddled around a central courtyard. Its artisans work in both traditional and modern styles, in silver filigree (for which Córdoba has long been famous), leather, wood and ceramics.

Picturesque lanes

Turn right at the top of the street, near the **Puerta de Almodóvar** ❿, part of the medieval city walls, and immediately right again down Calle Almanzor, which continues as Calle Romero. There are several restaurants down this street; two choice picks are **Casa El Churrasco** ❷ and **Casa Pepe de la Judería** ❸.

Turn left up Deanes and make a quick right down **Calle de La Hoquera**, an attractive street surviving from Muslim Córdoba. Turn left at the end, right at the square and right again down Velazquez Bosco, home to another Arab bathhouse, the **Banos Arabes de Santa Maria**. The first street on the left is **Calleja de las Flores** ⓫, one of Córdoba's prettiest streets, its houses adorned with flowerpots and ending in a small square.

Continue down Velazquez Bosco to reach the Mezquita.

LA MEZQUITA

Córdoba's most important monument, **La Mezquita** ⓬ (The Mosque; www.mezquita-catedraldecordoba.es; Mon–Sat Mar–Oct 10am–7pm, Nov–Feb 10am–6pm, Sun 8.30–11.30am and 3–6pm, Mar–Oct until 7pm; free Mon–Sat 8.30–9.30am; an additional ticket with a half-hour time slot is needed to go up the tower), is the oldest building in day-to-day use in the Western world. Its dominant feature is the 54-metre (177ft) bell tower, which has its origins in the 10th-century minaret; panoramic views can be enjoyed from the top.

Building the mosque

Construction of the Mezquita over the site of a Visigothic cathedral began in 786 at the order of Abd-al-Rahman I. The initial design was for an open courtyard (*sahn*) for ablutions, now known as the Patio de los Naranjos (orange trees), and a covered area that could accommodate as many as 10,000 worshippers. Three expansions later – by Abd-al-Rahman II in 833,

A detour to Medina Azahara is highly recommended

under al-Hakam II in 926, and finally by al-Mansur, who was chief minister of Hisham II, in 978 – it was completed.

The architectural style evolved with each addition, reaching the greatest splendour and technical mastery in what came to be known as the caliphal architectural style, during the Caliphate of al-Hakam. Features to note include the great skylighted domes (for extra interior light), and an ingenious engineering system comprising clustered pillars with intersecting lobed arches to support the domes.

After Fernando III reconquered Córdoba in 1236, small Christian chapels were added in 1258 and 1260. Nearly three centuries later, in 1523, during the reign of Carlos V, the Christian cathedral was built in the centre of the mosque. Whether inadvertent or not, the incongruous mix of architecture and culture combines to produce a place of utter fascination. Inside are hundreds of columns – 856 to be exact – most supporting double-horseshoe arches. The different coloured columns, fashioned from various types of stone, present a constantly mesmerising interplay of architecture and light.

Carlos V initiated the construction of the Christian cathedral inside the Mezquita. Later, however, he appeared to regret the decision, saying, 'Had I known what this was, you would not have done it, for what you are building here can be found anywhere; but what you have destroyed exists nowhere.'

Touring the mosque

Walking through the original mosque of Abd-al-Rahman I, you reach the Mezquita's first extension, added by Abd-al-Rahman II in 833 (a slight ramp in the floor is evidence of this being a later addition). To the left is the rear of the cathedral's *coro* (choir). Further on is the vaulted ceiling of an aborted church, planned in the 15th century. To the left

Medina Azahara

There is one important sight 7km (4.5 miles) outside Córdoba, in the foothills of the Sierra Morena. Medina Azahara (www.medinaazahara.org) was the handsome city-palace of Abd-al-Rahman III, now an extensive area of restored ruins including ornate horseshoe arches. The palace, reputedly built in honour of Abd-al-Rahman III's favourite concubine, the Syrian-born Al-Zahra or 'the Flower', was famous for its size and splendour. Its construction was said to have involved 10,000–12,000 workmen, and materials were brought from Constantinople as well as North Africa.

Despite its grandeur, the palace had a short life. After the breakup of the Caliphate of Córdoba early in the 11th century, it was utilised by various factions, then sacked. Many of the materials were used on constructions in Seville and other places and, over the next 900 years, it was allowed to fall into disrepair. Excavations began in 1910 and are ongoing.

Casa Pepe de La Judería

you will see the domed **Capilla de Villaviciosa**, where the old mosque's mihrab (indicating the direction of Mecca) would have been. Through a cutaway you can see the **Capilla Real** next door, redecorated in the 14th century in Mudéjar stucco. This was the mosque's *maqsura* (royal enclosure).

Food and Drink

① ALMUDAINA

Plaza Campo de los Santos Martires, 1; tel: 957-474 342; www.restaurante almudaina.com; L and D; €€€
Installed in a 15th century house near the Alcázar gardens, Almudaina serves local recipes based on fresh produce. Seven dining areas around a central courtyard.

② CASA EL CHURRASCO

Calle del Romero, 16; tel: 957-290 819; www.elchurrasco.com; L and D; €€€
The name suggests grilled meats, but there is much more besides. A good place to try *salmorejo*, a thick Córdoban version of gazpacho. Reservations advised.

③ CASA PEPE DE LA JUDERÍA

Calle del Romero, 1; tel: 957-200 744; http://restaurantecasapepedelajuderia. com; L and D; €€€
A typical Andalucían townhouse in the Judería with an interior courtyard. Decoration follows a bullfighting theme. There is a tapas bar here too.

Continuing straight ahead, you enter al-Hakam's extension. He extended the southern wall to the river and built an opulent new **mihrab** (seen through the railings), decorated with dazzling mosaics and a stunning star-ribbed dome that was subsequently copied throughout Spain. The bejewelled side rooms formed Hakam's *maqsura*.

The third extension of the Mezquita – by al-Mansur – is functional rather than aesthetically pleasing. It widened the prayer hall and courtyard to accommodate Córdoba's growing population.

Construction of the **cathedral** within the mosque required the removal of 60 of the original columns and some of the most beautiful stucco work. The contrast in styles is a jolt to the senses. In the cathedral, human images – taboo in Islamic art and architecture – abound in paint, stone and wood, particularly in the massive paintings of Christ and the saints.

The cathedral is of Gothic design, with later additions in plateresque and Baroque styles. Especially noteworthy are the mahogany choir stalls, carved by the Andalucían sculptor Pedro Duque Cornejo and depicting the lives of Jesus and the Virgin Mary in life-like detail. The magnificent golden altarpiece contains 36 tableaux of the *Life of Christ*.

Emerging from the mosque you can return to the starting point via Calle Torrijos.

Castillo de Santa Catalina   *Jaén Catedral*

JAÉN TO ÚBEDA

Far away from the coasts and the main tourist centres of Andalucía is the province of Jaén, an undulating sea of neatly spaced olive trees. Sited here are two of the most exquisite neighbouring towns in Spain, both jewels of Renaissance architecture.

DISTANCE: 56km (35 miles)
TIME: 1 day
START: Jaén city
END: Úbeda

The inland province of Jaén is known for its vast olive groves – there are around 40 million trees here – creating a landscape that is rhythmically enchanting. Most people hurry through this area, but it is worth taking the time to stop and explore properly. This route starts in the provincial capital of Jaén before taking a short drive to the two historic towns of Úbeda and Baeza. Allow time for three highly rewarding urban walks.

JAÉN CITY

The city of **Jaén** ❶, perched halfway up a hillside, makes a good jumping-off point. Its monuments are clustered in the upper part of the city. They include the Renaissance **Catedral** (Mon–Fri 10am–2pm and 4–8pm, Sat 10am–2pm and 4–7pm, Sun 10am–noon and 4–7pm),

which claims to possess one of the three cloths in Christendom indelibly stamped with the face of Jesus Christ after being used by Veronica to wipe the sweat from his face as he went towards his crucifixion. Beneath the **Palacio de Villardompardo**, a 16th-century mansion, is a complete suite of Arab baths, the **Baños Arabes** (www.bañosarabesjaen.es; Tue–Sat 9am–10pm, Sun 9am–3pm; free). These are the largest and best-restored of their kind in Spain, their chambers divided by horseshoe arches and lit by star-shaped skylights. The other building to see is right at the top of the hill, the **Castillo de Santa Catalina**, an Arab castle with spectacular views. Beside it is a parador hotel (see page 110).

BEAUTIFUL BAEZA

From Jaén it's an easy drive along the A316 motorway, crossing the River Guadalquivir, to **Baeza** ❷. The town's splendid honey-coloured palaces, churches and civic buildings, dating largely from the wealthy 15th to 17th centuries, have a cherished rather than lived-in

air, as if history had left them frozen in their glory days. Its historic centre is so compact that you could walk around it in half an hour, although it deserves a far more leisurely visit.

Plaza del Pópulo

The natural starting point for a stroll is the little square off the bottom of the large Plaza de la Constitución (the best place to park, if you can), the **Plaza del Pópulo**, also called the Plaza de los Leones after the lion fountain in the middle, built using stone from the ruined Roman town of Cástulo. At the head of this square is the **Casa del Pópulo**, containing the tourist information office and beside it two monumental gateways, the **Puerta de Jaén** and the **Arco de Villalar**.

The other handsome Renaissance building on the square, the **Antigua Carnicería**, was built as Baeza's slaughterhouse or butcher's shop.

Catedral and Palacio de Japalquinto

Head uphill and bear left to reach the **Catedral** (Mon–Fri 10.30am–2pm and 4–6pm, Sat 10.30am–6pm, Sun 10.30am–5pm), remodelled in the 16th century but including some of its earlier Gothic elements. Its main door looks down onto a quiet cobbled square surrounding a quaint triumphal arch of a fountain, the **Fuente de Santa María**. The former Seminario de San Felipe Neri opposite the cathedral (on the lower side of the square) is adorned with the fading red calligraphic *vitores* dating from between 1668 and 1720: graffiti by former students of the school in praise of someone or something of their fancy.

Downhill to the right of the seminary is Baeza's finest building, the **Palacio de Jabalquinto** (patio only: Mon–Fri 9am–2pm; free), which has a decorative Isabelline facade framed by two pillars and topped by a gallery of arches. At the bottom of the slope you emerge on the Paseo de la Constitución. Across this and one street back is the **Ayuntamiento** (Town Hall), once used as an old prison, which has ornate window surrounds on its upper floor.

There is a highly regarded restaurant specialising in olive oil just outside town, **Juanito** ❶.

ELEGANT ÚBEDA

A stone's throw from Baeza, on an adjacent hill and reachable either by motorway or a connecting main road, is **Úbeda** ❸, where a group of monumental palaces and churches forms the core of a modern town. The ensemble is largely the work of architect Andrés de Vandelvira, under the patronage of two noblemen, Francisco de los Cobos and his nephew Juan Vázquez de Molina, both powerful and ambitious secretaries to the emperor of Spain.

With a few exceptions, all the buildings worth seeing are contained within the area circumscribed by the old city walls (of which only fragments remain), mak-

Lundscaped gardens at the Plaza de Vázquez de Molina

ing Úbeda better to explore on foot than by car; there's a car park in the Plaza de Andalucía, just outside the walls.

Plazas del Ayuntamiento and de Vázquez de Molina

From here, walk down Calle Real into the monumental area and the **Plaza del Ayuntamiento**, on which stands the town hall, the Palacio de las Cadenas and a good restaurant, **Mesón Navarro**, see ❷. Off a corner of the square is the **Palacio Vela de los Cobos** (guided tours only), which has a gallery of arches along its top floor ending with a white marble column in one corner.

Behind the Palacio de las Cadenas is the adjacent square of **Plaza de Vázquez de Molin**, an open-plan public space planted with clipped hedges and ornamental trees. This is the centrepiece of Úbeda's network of small streets and magnificent buildings. At one end of the square stands the domed chapel **Sacra Capilla El Salvador** (www.fundacionmedinaceli.org; Mon–Thu 9.30am–2.30pm and 4.30–7pm, Fri and Sat 9.30am–3pm and 4.30–7.30pm, Sun 11.30am–3pm and 4.30–7.30pm), commissioned by Francisco de los Cobos as a family pantheon with an extravagant interior. The north side of the square is formed by two other imposing buildings, the former Dean of Málaga's residence, converted into a parador (see page 110), which has a delightful patio, and the **Palacio Vázquez de Molina** (Mon–Fri 8am–2.30pm; free), by Vandelvira, now the Town Hall. On the other side of the square are the **Antiguo Pósito** (the Old Granary) and, set back a little, **Santa María de los Reales Alcázares** (daily, times vary). This large church is mainly 13th century, incorporating part of an old mosque and fortress with a conspicuous Renaissance facade.

Beyond Plaza de Vázquez de Molina

There are a great many other remarkable buildings to discover in the streets of Úbeda, but it's not easy to link them up in a coherent pattern. The best thing to do is use the Plaza de Vázquez de Molina as a point of reference and make excur-

Sinagoga del Agua

sions towards the compass points. To the east and south you can't get far because you quickly pass through the city walls and are faced with an endless vista of olive trees.

West of the square is the **Casa Museo Arte Andalusí** (Calle Navarez, 11; daily 11.30am–2pm and 5–8pm), a private museum housed in a 16th-century palace and containing an interesting collection of the owner's Spanish and Moroccan antiques. The nearby **Casa de las Torres** is an early 16th-century mansion with a plateresque facade framed by two towers.

To the north of the square is the **Sinagoga del Agua** (Calle Roque Rojas 2; daily 10.30am–2pm and 5.30–8.30pm, guided tours lasting 30 minutes only), a synagogue and rabbi's house dating from (at least) the 14th century. These important remains were only discovered when a local businessman bought and began renovating adjoining buildings to turn into shops and flats. Close by you'll find the **Iglesia de San Pablo**, a 13th-century church with a Gothic southern door and a Romanesque westerly door. In the square outside there is a monument to St John of the Cross, who died in Úbeda in 1591. There is a **museum** (Calle del Carmen 13; www.sanjuandelacruzubeda.com; Tue–Sun 11am–2pm and 4.30–6.30pm) dedicated to the saint just east of here.

Food and Drink

🅠 JUANITO

Puche Pardo 57 Baeza; tel: 953-740 040; http://www.juanitobaeza.com; L and D, closed Sun and Mon evening; €€€

Juanito's location – next to a petrol station on the road to Úbeda – may not look promising, but this is a highly renowned restaurant that has entertained politicians, bullfighters and royalty. It is the place to come if you are at least curious about olive oil: a trolley of 20 or more varieties will be brought to your table.

🅡 MESÓN NAVARRO

Plaza del Ayuntamiento, 2 Úbeda; tel: 953-757 395; L; €€

Centrally located in the historic part of town, and serving a good-value *menú del día*. If you happen to overshoot lunchtime, many items on the menu – including meats, salads and seafood – are available as tapas and *raciones* at the bar. A good place to try the local cuisine.

Centro de Interpretación Olivar y Aceite
It's well worth leaving the old part of the town to explore the local olive-oil industry. Make for the well-executed **Centro de Interpretación Olivar y Aceite** (Corredera San Francisco 32; www.centrodeolivaryaceite.com; June–Sept Tue–Sat 10am–1pm and 6–9pm, Sun 10am–1pm, Oct–May Tue–Sat 11am–2pm and 5–8pm, Sun 11am–2pm) just outside the northern walls.

Río Borosa walking trail

THROUGH THE SIERRA DE CAZORLA

Destress yourself with this antidote to all coasts and cities: a magnificent drive through forested mountain nature reserve, using the magnificent town of Úbeda as the start and end point.

DISTANCE: 180km (112 miles)
TIME: 1 day
START & END: Úbeda
POINTS TO NOTE: This is quite a long drive for one day so make an early start or stay at a hotel along the way (see page 110). There are few towns on this route so carry provisions or plan a lunch stop in advance.

This tour is a long loop through the beautiful countryside of inland Andalucía.

CAZORLA TOWN

From **Úbeda ❶**, take the N322 to Torreperogil and turn on to the N315 to Peal de Becerra. Although it's not obvious, you pass a nature reserve – the Puente de La Cerrada, with pairs of breeding waterfowl – on the way. At Peal de Becerro, you may want to make a short detour to visit the impressive excavated Iberian burial chamber of Toya – it's only about 5km (3 miles) out of town, but make sure to ask Peal town hall for the keys before setting off.

From Peal, turn on to the N319 to reach the town of **Cazorla ❷**, the best access point for exploring the forested limestone ridges and deep, steep valleys of the **Parque Natural de las Sierras de Cazorla, Segura y Las Villas**, Spain's largest nature and game reserve. It makes up almost one-fifth of the province of Jaén. The new 479km (297-mile) GR247 footpath passes through the park in 21 stages.

Cazorla itself clings to a steep slope under a rocky ridge, looking out onto an endless sea of olive trees. Its heart is the Plaza de la Corredera, popularly known as 'El Huevo' because it is shaped like an egg. Take the opportunity to buy provisions here – or patronise **Las Vagas**, see ❶ – and fill up with fuel (this is the last town you'll see for a while). In summer there's also a choice of terrace cafés in the Plaza de Santa María.

An Iberian ibex

INTO THE NATURE RESERVE

Leave Cazorla, following the brown signs for 'Parque Natural' ('nature reserve'). Soon you pass under the Templar castle of **La Iruela**, which stands dramatically on an outcrop of rock. The road traverses Burunchel before gaining height to cross over a wooded pass, the Puerto de Palomas (1,138 metres/3,733ft).

There are two *miradores* (viewpoints) at the top. The Paso del Aire, on the right, overlooks the olive groves to the northwest. The **Mirador de Puerto de las Palomas**, however, a little further on, gives an overview of the dense woods of the Guadalquivir valley at the heart of the reserve.

Come down through the trees to reach a crossroads, the Empalme de la Valle. If you've got plenty of time you can make a detour up to the **Parador de Cazorla** (see page 110) or go in search of the source of the Guadalquivir (a round trip of almost 40 km/25 miles from the crossroads).

Otherwise, turn left to take the A319 along the valley, towards Torre del Vinagre. You cross the Guadalquivir twice, but it is still only a stream; there's no hint that it will become the most important river in Andalucía.

Torre del Vinagre

The **Torre del Vinagre** ❸ (daily 10am–2pm and 4–8pm, winter until 6pm) is a visitor centre with exhibitions about the habitats of the surrounding valleys and mountains. Apart from its importance in terms of wildlife preservation – the reserve has a rich population of eagles and vultures among other birds – it has many endemic species of plant. Hunting of certain species is permitted here, but under strictly controlled circumstances. It's certainly become less common in the days since dictator General Franco came to Cazorla in 1959 and bagged a record-breaking deer. There is a botanical garden across the road from the Torre del Vinagre, and a nearby fish farm with information about aquatic life.

There are a few restaurants around the small settlement of Coto Rios.

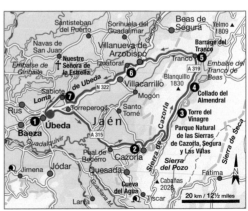

The Guadalquivir valley is Andalucía's most fertile area

There's not much to choose, from but the **Hotel Mirasierra** ❷ will provide you with a straightforward mountain meal.

Collado del Almendral

As you continue down the valley, look out for a sign reading 'Parque Cinegetico', marking an area called the **Collado del Almendral** ❹. Park here or a little further on and follow the footpath to see deer kept in large enclosures. If you have the stamina, continue to the top of the hill for fine views.

The road now winds around the reservoir of El Tranco and crosses a **dam** ❺. Traffic across the dam is regulated by a lonely traffic light. If you really want to get off the beaten track you can detour to visit the impressively sited fortress town of Segura de la Sierra, some way beyond the head of the lake – then find your way across country to the N322 to resume the route; this will involve a lot of extra driving. Simpler is to turn left immediately across the dam on to the A5202 for Villanueva del Arzobispo. This road climbs through and eventually out of a delightful gorge.

Iznatoraf and Sabiote

Turn left towards Úbeda when you meet the N322, keeping a look out for the right turn to **Iznatoraf** ❻. The town is built around a 16th-century church and several gateways survive from its medieval Arab wall. The main reason to come here, however, is to take in the endless views back to Cazorla and La Iruela, and ahead to Sabiote. To the northwest is the Sierra Morena, separating Andalucía from Castile.

Go back to the N322 and continue south until you see a sign for **Sabiote** ❼. There are some beautiful old streets lined with well-to-do houses spreading up the hill between its castle (Moorish but treated to a Renaissance facelift) and the town hall. Most of the medieval walls are still standing, pierced by six gateways.

A direct road, the A6103, takes you back to Úbeda.

Food and Drink

❶ LAS VEGAS
Plaza de la Corredera 17, Cazorla; tel: 669-553 068; www.turismoencazorla.com/bar/lasvegas.html; B, L and D; €
Don't expect glamour in this bar on the main square of Cazorla, but do come for great tapas and ingredients that you won't find on the coast. Here the emphasis is on local game, freshwater fish and mushrooms, all prepared using 'Jaen gold' – cold pressed virgin extra olive oil.

❷ HOTEL MIRASIERRA
Carretera A319 Km 51. Coto Rios; tel: 953-713 044; www.mirasierrahotel.es/; L and D; €
It is worth stopping at this roadside hotel-restaurant for a meal if you are not too demanding about your surroundings.

Bold colours grace Plaza Nueva

GRANADA CITY CENTRE AND ALBAICÍN

The last city to fall to the Reconquest, Granada is steeped in history. This route explores the main sights of the city centre and the labyrinthine old Moorish quarter of the Albaicín, whose main square gives a dazzling view of the Alhambra.

DISTANCE: 2.5km (1.5 miles)
TIME: 1 day
START: Catedral
END: Plaza Nueva
POINTS TO NOTE: The route is short but involves a steep ascent.

The Alhambra is the prize draw of Granada, but the city centre has other monuments, too. This route begins in the city's heart, before climbing to the Moorish quarter of the Albaicín, a delightful huddle of houses and secretive patio-gardens.

CITY CENTRE SIGHTS

Catedral and around

Rising out of the hubbub of central Granada is the **Catedral ❶** (Mon–Sat 10am–6.30pm, Sun 3–6pm), built on the site of the main mosque and one of the most important examples of Renaissance architecture in Spain. The warm, honey-coloured exterior contrasts with the austere interior.

Next to the cathedral, accessed from Calle Oficios, is the appealing **Capilla Real** (Royal Chapel; www.capillarealgranada. com; Mon–Sat 10.15am–6.30pm, Sun 11am–6.30pm), the mausoleum of the so-called 'Catholic Monarchs', Fernando and Isabel. The black-lead coffins of this famously pious and proactive double act are on public display in the crypt, along with those of their luckless daughter, remembered by history as Juana the Mad, and her philandering husband, Felipe the Fair. Above the family vault, the chapel has superb iron grillework and a lavish Baroque altarpiece. The sacristy, on the way out, houses an exquisite collection of primitive Flemish paintings.

Across the street from the chapel is the **Madraza**, the Arab university founded in the 14th century by Yusuf I, of which only the oratory remains from the original building (across the patio on the left); its intricate Arabic decoration was covered over for centuries, only to be rediscovered under a layer of plaster in 1893.

Next to the Madraza, go through **the Alcaicería**, a warren of souvenir shops designed to resemble an Arab souk, to

Heading up to the Albaicín   *Arabic market, Albaicín*

reach central Granada's main traffic artery, the Calle Reyes de Católicos, which intersects with the Gran Vía de Colón at Plaza de Isabel La Católica, dominated by a statue of Queen Isabel receiving Columbus.

Across Reyes Católicos is the attractive **Corral del Carbón ❷** (daily 9am–8pm; free), built as an inn in the 14th century but later used as a theatre and coal depot.

Plaza Nueva

Go up Reyes Católicos and cross Plaza de Isabel La Católica to reach the large busy square of **Plaza Nueva ❸**, on which stands the Real Chancillería (Royal Chancellery), built in 1530. The tourist information office can be found beside the Iglesia de Santa Ana.

THE ALBAICÍN

Take the street leaving the bottom of the square, Calle Elvira. (Down the first street to your left is **Bodegas Castañeda**, see ❶, one of Granada's classic tapas bars, if you need to refuel). Turn right up Calle Calderería Vieja, lined with craft shops.

At the top of the street you are in the thick of the Albaicín, a network of steep erratic streets, steps and alleyways. It's tempting to follow your fancy here; don't worry if you stray off the route and get lost along the way – just head back downhill and regain your bearings at the bottom.

Turn right to reach Plaza San Gregorio, continuing up to Cuesta San Gregorio to take the first little street to the

left to reach **Placeta de San José ❹**. From here, continue on Calle San José, which goes steeply upwards. Ahead of you is the lovely 10th-century minaret of San José. Head uphill underneath this and you'll soon come to the handsome doorway of the Carmen San Luís. This is a good example of the magnificent mansion-patio complexes known as *cármenes* built by the city's well to do. Most, unfortunately, are private and closed to the public.

Continue up the hill to reach **Placeta de San**

Bodegas Castañeda is well liked by locals and visitors

Miguel Bajo ❺, overlooked by a white-washed church. In the corner of the square is a 13th-century Moorish cistern testifying to an ingenious system of water collection and storage that kept the gardens of the Albaicín green even in summer.

Follow the Calle Santa Isabel la Real along the hill, passing a 16th- to 17th-century convent. Ahead is the white tower of the Igelsia de San Nicolás. Immediately beneath it is a square and the **Mirador de San Nicolás** ❻, a famed viewpoint looking directly across the Darro valley at the Alhambra.

Coming back down

There are various ways to get down from the Albaicín; the streets and squares are intricately meshed, so don't worry if you get lost. Keeping going downhill. If you can see the Alhambra in front of you, you're heading in the right direction.

Leave the Mirador de San Nicolas on the short, steep, stepped road beneath it, the Cuesta de las Cabras. Turn left in front of the mosque. At the end of the street, round the corner to your right and fork left on to the sloping Cuesta de las Tomases. You will soon reach the Placeta del Comino and the 15th-century Carmen de Aben Humeya. A little further down is the quaintly shaped **Placeta del Aljibe de Trillo**, named after an old water cistern. Turn left down Calle Guinea and take the first right to emerge in Plaza Escuelas, on which stands the Iglesia de San Juan de los Reyes. Carry on directly downhill via Calle Zafra to emerge on the street running beside the River Darro. On your left is the **Casa de Castril**, housing the Archaeology Museum (tel: 600-143 141; summer Tue–Sat 9am–3pm, winter Tue–Sat 9am–9pm, Sun 9am–3pm; currently closed for renovations).

ALONG THE RIVER

Turn right along the river (Carrera del Darro) in front of the 16th century Convento de Santa Catalina, where nuns sell cakes over a Lazy Susan. There is a ruined half-arch (Moorish) hovering above the river to the left. Not far on is **El Bañuelo** ❼ (daily May–mid-Sept 10am–2.30pm and 5–8.30pm, mid-Sept–Apr 10am–5pm; free Sun), an 11th-century Moorish bath-house with vaulted interiors lit by skylights in the shape of small stars.

If you've built up an appetite, visit **La Fontana**, see ❷, or continue back to Plaza Nueva.

Food and Drink

❶ BODEGAS CASTAÑEDA

Almireceros 1–3; tel: 958-215 464; tapas; €
One of Granada's classic tapas bars, Bodegas Castañeda trades on its reputation and is hugely popular.

❷ LA FONTANA

Carrera del Darro 19; tel: 958-049 449; http://barlafontana.com; B, L and D; €
Open from 9am to 1am, serving breakfast, tapas, sandwiches, salads and full meals.

La Fontana

THE ALHAMBRA

The fortress-palace of the Alhambra is one of the wonders of the world, the apogee of the Muslim civilisation in Spain. Its austere exterior is softened by its exquisitely decorated interior and the magnificent water gardens of the Generalife.

DISTANCE: 3.5km (2 miles)
TIME: Half a day
START: Puerta de las Granadas
END: Palacio de Carlos V
POINTS TO NOTE: The Alhambra is open daily year-round 8.30am–6pm. Booking ahead (tel: 902-888 001; http://tickets.alhambra-patronato.es) is highly recommended; you can buy on the day at the ticket office (open from 8am), but they sell out quickly. Advanced tickets can be picked up, using the same credit card, from ticket machines at the Alhambra or from the cash machines at any branch of La Caixa bank in Andalucía. Only 300 visitors are admitted to the Nasrid Palaces every 30 minutes; choose a time slot to suit you, which will be shown on your ticket. While waiting you can visit other parts of the complex. You can take food and drink into the Alhambra, but only eat in a designated place. Parking is plentiful but expensive; you can also walk up or take bus C3 or C4 from Plaza Isabel La Católica.

INTRODUCTION TO THE ALHAMBRA

Everything else in Granada – indeed in Andalucía – is a foretaste for the one building everyone comes to the city to see, the **Alhambra**. No other monument in Spain has exerted such fascination over travellers and historians over the centuries, or inspired so many poets, composers, painters and writers.

The road to preservation

That the palace-fortress, its gardens and the summer residence, the Generalife, can still be termed 'the best-preserved medieval Arab palace in the world' is nothing short of a miracle given the Alhambra's history. An earthquake in 1522 and an explosion in 1590 caused significant damage. During the Peninsular War, Napoleonic troops used the Alhambra as a garrison and destroyed part of its ramparts. Further destruction was undertaken in 1626 by Carlos I (known as Emperor Charles V outside Spain), who decided to build a palace in the confines of the Alham-

bra in a style of jarring incongruity. Then, 50 years later, the palace's mosque was knocked down to make way for the Church of Santa María.

It was largely thanks to the 'discovery' of the Alhambra by 19th-century writers and artists – among them, Gustave Doré, Victor Hugo, Washington Irving and Mérimée – that the monument was at last recognised as unique. In 1870 the Alhambra was declared a national monument and restoration began, although the first efforts were geared more to creating the ideal image of a fairy-tale castle as envisioned by the romantics of the day than a faithful recreation of the building. It wasn't until the 1920s that a measure of historical rigour was applied to the restoration, a painstaking process that continues to this day, carried out by a permanent staff of architects and craftsmen.

Form and function

The Alhambra is made up of three principal parts: the Royal Palace, the Alcazaba (or fortress) and the Medina, where up to 2,000 members of the royal household lived, but which today is mainly given over to gardens. Further up the slope stands a fourth part of the complex, the summer palace of the rulers of Granada, the Generalife.

The Alhambra largely dates from the 14th century, but it is better thought of as an accumulation of buildings over time. When in 1238 Muhammad Ben Nasr founded the Nasrid dynasty that was to rule Granada until 1492, he held court in a castle where today's Alcazaba stands. It wasn't until his descendant Yusuf I became king 100 years later that building on the new palace began. The reign of this Nasrid king, and that of his son Muhammad V, which together lasted from 1333 to 1391, saw the construction of all the most important elements of the royal palace as we know them today.

The core of the Alhambra is the Royal Palace (the Casa Real or Palacios Nazaries), a fantasy of delicate arches, intricate carving and trickling fountains. Unlike the self-confident grandeur of the Mezquita in Córdoba, or the restrained elegance of the Almohads' Giralda in Seville, the Alhambra has an almost ephemeral quality, and, indeed, the carved patterns and inscriptions on plaster which are the most striking decorative feature were regarded as no more permanent than today's wallpaper; successive rulers would remove the work of their predecessors and have it replaced with inscriptions more to their liking.

Built with clay bricks, mortar and wood, the whole palace is the architectural expression of a civilisation in its twilight years, when the once formidable military might of Muslim Spain had been replaced by the intense, if relatively brief, cultural flowering of Nasrid Granada.

The intrigues that unfolded in the rooms of the Royal Palace, pitting the sultan Mulay Hassan and his favourite concubine, the Christian-born Zoraya, against his wife Aixa and their luckless

The breathtaking Alhambra

son Boabdil, would spark a civil war and precipitate Granada's eventual downfall.

ENTRANCE

If your legs and lungs are up to it, it's well worth starting out from the **Plaza Nueva**, at the foot of the Alhambra hill in central Granada, and walking up the shaded Cuesta de Gomérez and through the **Puerta de las Granadas ❶** (Gate of the Pomegranates), built on Carlos I's orders in 1536. It is decorated with three pomegranates, symbol of the city (the Spanish word for pomegranate is *granada*, although the city's name has a different origin; it comes from the name given to

the city by its sizeable Jewish population during Visigoth days, Garnatha).

As you approach the Alhambra, on the left-hand side you'll see the impressive **Puerta de la Justicia ❷** (Gate of Justice or Bib Xaria), one of the main entrances to the palace, on which are engraved the Islamic symbols of a hand and a key. As every tour guide will tell you, the Moorish legend insisted that Christian visitors would never enter this gate until the hand reached down to grasp the key.

ALCAZABA

The Puerta de la Justicia leads you into the **Plaza de los Aljibes**. This square

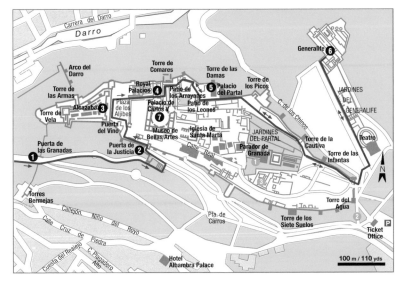

Tranquil Patio de Comares

commands the first of many magnificent views over the Albaicín and Sacromonte. If you have half an hour to spare before your allotted time in the Royal Palace, tour the **Alcazaba** ❸ now, the military area of the Alhambra. (If you visit later, its stark military aspect may come as an anti-climax after the splendour of the Nasrid Palaces.) The massive fortress juts out like the prow of a ship on the Alhambra hill.

Make your way across the **Plaza de Armas** (which has a small snack bar selling beers, sandwiches and soft drinks), where you can view the foundations of the soldiers' domestic quarters, and climb up to the **Torre de Vela**. Isabel had a bell installed in this tower after the fall of Granada to symbolise the Christian triumph (bells are banned under Islam).

One last stop before the Nasrid palaces is the illuminating **Sala de Presentación**, in a Moorish *aljibe* (water cistern) under the Palace of Carlos, an introduction to the Alhambra covering both its history and the techniques and materials used in its construction.

NASRID PALACES

The **Royal Palace** ❹ (Palacios Nazaries), the highlight of the visit, comprises three distinct parts, leading from the most public areas to the most private quarters, ending up with a visit to the baths or *hammam*. Inside the entrance to the palace is the *mexuar*, where citizens of Granada were received and justice was meted out; from here, you enter the *serail*, where official, diplomatic life took place; and finally, the *harem*, the monarch's private quarters.

Mexuar

The *mexuar* is not as well preserved as the rest of the palace, having been converted into a chapel shortly after the expulsion of the Moorish court and also damaged by the 1590 explosion. At the end of the main room is an oratory with a glimpse of the intricate geometrical motifs so prolific elsewhere.

Serail

From here a small courtyard (Patio del Mexuar) leads to the **Cuarto Dorado** (Golden Room), where the sultan's visitors were received. The entrance to the *serail*, through the left-hand door at the end of the patio, follows a zigzag route, thus protecting its access. Within this part of the palace diplomatic life was intense, especially in the latter half of the 14th century when the power of the Moors in Spain was draining away. Central to this part of the Alhambra is the **Patio de Comares** (also called Patio de los Arrayanes/Courtyard of the Myrtles), which, with the reflection of the buildings in the water of the pool, is an outstanding example of the symmetry of Islamic art. Critics refer to this as 'the Parthenon of Arab art in Spain'.

At one end of this patio is the **Torre de Comares**, in the ground floor of

Patio de los Leones   *Picture-postcard Palacio del Partal*

which is the majestic **Salón de Embajadores** (Ambassadors' Hall), perhaps the room which leaves the most lasting impression on visitors. The domed ceiling, representing the firmament, is inlaid with cedar and reaches a height of over 15 metres (50ft). The sultan used to sit with his back to the light, facing entering visitors, thus keeping an advantage over them.

Harem

From the Patio de Comares you pass into the *harem*, accessed from the **Patio de los Leones** (Patio of the Lions). The domestic quarters of the sultan, his wives and the sultan's mother (a key figure in Moorish court life) lead off this central courtyard – the **Sala de los Reyes** (Hall of the Kings), the **Sala de los Abencerrajes** (Hall of the Abencerrajes) and the **Sala de las Dos Hermanas** (Hall of the Two Sisters).

Amid the overwhelming richness of the *harem* as a whole, several architectural and decorative features are distinctive. First there is the anti-earthquake device, a lead plate inserted at the top of the 124 white-marble pillars. Next, the 12 lions themselves, surrounding the central fountain: according to one theory, the lions represent the Twelve Tribes of Israel, and the two marked with an equilateral triangle on the forehead symbolise the Chosen Tribes.

The paintings on leather in the Sala de los Reyes, where human figures appear, were probably done by Castilian artists who sought refuge in Granada from the reign of terror of Pedro the Cruel. Look for the traces of 'blood' in the fountain in the Sala de los Abencerrajes, 'proof' of the veracity of the legend which tells of how 36 members of the Abencerraje family (Boabdil's family's rival clan) were beheaded one by one as they entered – a sultan's revenge for his mistress's infidelity.

Exit the patio via the Sala de las Dos Hermanas, with its cupola said to be decorated with more than 5,000 cavities, to reach the **Baño de Comares** (Royal Baths), titled chambers with star-spangled domed roofs. From here you can wander down to the area where the 19th-century American author Washington Irving lived in 'delicious thraldom' while writing his bestseller *Tales of the Alhambra*.

PARTAL AND MEDINA

Leaving the palaces you cross an open area of quiet gardens flanked by the **Palacio del Partal** ❺ (the oldest part of the complex) and unrestored parts of the exterior walls. It is overlooked by the Parador hotel (see page 94).

GENERALIFE

Keep going in this direction towards the Nasrids' summer palace, the **Generalife** ❻. The likeliest explanation for the name Generalife is that it derives

Palacio de Carlos V

from the Arabic *Gennet al-Arif* ('architect's garden'), because it is not the palace that's the main draw, but its gardens – perhaps the most magnificent in Spain. They are all that remain of what was once a much larger estate. The River Darro was diverted 18km (11 miles) to feed this oasis of fountains and waterfalls.

The sound of running water is particularly soothing for anyone who has had enough of heat and monuments, although it is questionable whether the Italianate layout of the present gardens owes anything to the Moors, who were more interested in roses, aromatic herbs and fruit and vegetables than in trimmed cypress hedges.

Only a part of the palace remains but it blends harmoniously into the gardens. It includes the **Patio de la Acequia**, with its long and narrow central pond flanked by water spouts, and the **Patio de los Cipreses** (Courtyard of the Cypresses). Despite the name, there is only one cypress tree here now, the dead trunk of a venerable tree that was supposedly witness to the illicit encounters between Zoraya, the sultan's concubine, and her Abencerraje lover, a liaison that led to the massacre of the Abencerraje family in the Sala de los Abencerrajes. Ascending from here is the **Escalera de Agua**, a stairway whose banisters hold channels of rushing water.

PALACIO DE CARLOS V

There is one more part of the Alhambra complex that you might want to visit if you have the time (and energy). Retrace your steps through the Jardines del Partal to the **Palacio de Carlos V** ❼, an addition to the Alhambra built on the orders of the eponymous king. It is glaringly out of place among the Nasrid architecture, but is still one of the most outstanding examples of Renaissance architecture in Spain, with its unique circle-within-a-square layout.

After visiting the Alhambra, head to the **Parador de Granada** ❶ or **La Mimbre**, ❷ to sate your appetite.

Food and Drink

❶ **PARADOR DE GRANADA**
Real de la Alhambra; tel: 958-221 440; www.parador.es; L and D; €€€
This prestigious hotel is an exclusive place to stay, but anyone can come and eat here. The formal restaurant serves exquisite regional cuisine but there is a more relaxed bar where you can order a snack (€).

❷ **LA MIMBRE**
Avenida del Generalife; tel: 958-222 276; www.restaurantelamimbre.es; L and D; €€
This is a small restaurant in an unbeatable location at the very foot of the Alhambra walls, with outdoor dining on a shaded terrace in summer. Traditional Granada dishes.

The Poqueira valley

THE ALPUJARRAS

Over the Sierra Nevada from Granada is one of Spain's most charming corners: the deep, leafy mountain slopes and valleys of the Alpujarras. This trip takes you through them and finishes with a visit to the extraordinary subterranean suburb of Guadix.

DISTANCE: 137km (85 miles)
TIME: 2 days
START & END: Granada
POINTS TO NOTE: Overnight at one of the hotels along the way (see page 111). Don't attempt this route in winter; even in late autumn and early spring you should check the Puerto de la Ragua is open before setting off.

Once a poor, remote and self-contained world of its own, the gigantic mountainsides and plunging valleys of Las Alpujarras first became known to the world in the 1950s because of a book written by Gerald Brenan, an English intellectual, who had taken refuge there from civilisation 30 years before.

GRANADA TO ÓRGIVA

Leave **Granada ❶** on the motorway heading for the Costa Tropical, the A44. Turn off on to the A348 for the spa of **Lanjarón ❷**, which has turned its spring water into one of Spain's most popular bottled brands. Its one monument – the ruins of a Moorish castle on a rock adrift from the rest of Lanjarón – can be seen from the ring-road as you drive around the bottom of town.

The road descends towards **Órgiva ❸**, the main service town of the western Alpujarras, but you don't need to go into it. Instead, turn left onto the A4132 at the junction immediately before it, towards Trevélez and Pitres.

THE POQUEIRA VALLEY

Climbing further into the mountains, you pass two typical Alpujarran villages, Carataunas and Soportújar, before at last rounding a corner and entering a deep ravine, the Barranco de Poqueira, the most scenic and visited part of the Alpujarras.

It contains three villages spaced out on the south-facing hillside. Don't attempt to navigate the villages of the Alpujarras in a car: park outside and explore on foot. The houses are built as if at random. This creates higgledy-piggledy street patterns of shaded, narrow lanes and alleys widening and constricting again for no appar-

Trevélez

ent reason, and often stepped or ribbed to prevent pedestrians and pack-mules slipping on a frosty day.

Pampaneira

The first (and lowest of the three) is **Pampaneira**; have a stroll around before you resume the journey. As you pass above the village you will now see one of the most characteristic features of the local architecture: flat, gravel-spread roofs on a variety of levels sprouting improbably shaped chimneys with washing lines attached to them.

Capileira

The road twists and climbs out of the deepest part of the valley and comes to a junction. Turn left on the A4129 to reach the two higher villages of Bubión and **Capileira** ❹, the latter perhaps the best-kept and most picturesque of all those in the Alpujarras.

If you're in the mood for a walk, follow your nose out of any of the villages – up, down or along the slope – to get an idea of how people lived in pre-modern times. The farms of the Alpujarras were laid out as a series of terraces, and while some are disused and overgrown, many are still cultivated using the same system of gurgling

irrigation channels as the Moors used 500 years ago to conserve the melt water coming down from the Sierra Nevada. You may also come across a threshing floor – a flat disk of stones that was essential to village life before machinery. The smattering of mulberry trees is a direct legacy of the Alpujarras' silk industry of old – mulberry leaves being the food of the fussy silkworm.

Beyond Capileira, the road continues over the top of the Sierra Nevada to the ski resort above Granada, which is unfortunately closed to traffic. You can, however, take a minibus from the Sierra Nevada National Park visitor centre above Capileira to the higher slopes and climb to the summit of the Mulhacén (3,478 metres/11,411ft), the highest mountain in the Iberian peninsula.

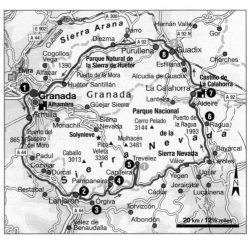

Cave houses, Guadix

TREVÉLEZ

Return to the junction and continue along the A4132. The road passes through Pitres, Pórtugos and Busquistar, before swinging into a large valley at the head of which stands **Trevélez ❺**.

Trevélez is the highest village in Spain, sited at 1,476 metres (4,843ft). It puts its altitude to good use for the dry-curing of hams; buy some at La Ruta de Trevélez (Pisto del Barrio Medio 19; www.jamonescanogonzalez.com). Although the lower part of this village seems like one big tourist shop, the two upper parts *(barrios)* have retained some authenticity. There are several places to eat in Trevélez; one good option is **La Fragua**, see ❶.

ACROSS PUERTO DE LA RAGUA

After Trevélez the road passes through a string of other Alpujarreno villages including Yegen – where Gerald Brenan lived – before turning north and crossing the mountains via the **Puerto de la Ragua ❻**, a 2,000-metre (6,562ft) pass. There are good views as you descend. Below the pass is the **Castillo de La Calahorra ❼**, an early 16th-century Renaissance castle with a cylindrical tower at each of the four corners.

Guadix

Join the A92 motorway heading in the direction of Granada, but turn off almost immediately for **Guadix ❽**. The city cen-

tre has several monuments, but most people come to visit the Barrio de Cuevas. The houses initially appear indistinguishable from ordinary homes; look closely, though, and the white, circular chimneys emanating from the rocks give the game away. These are actually cave houses with a practical use: they're cool in summer and warm in winter. There's a cave museum near the church, but for an aerial view of the cave quarter follow the signs for the 'Mirador Cerro de las Balas'. Head for **La Bodeguilla ❷** in town for something to eat.

Return to Granada via the A92 motorway, stopping in Purullena to pick up some traditional pottery as a souvenir or gift.

Food and Drink

❶ LA FRAGUA
Calle San Antonio, 4, Trevélez; tel: 958-858 573; www.hotellafragua.com; L and D; €€
Situated next to the town hall, with fine views from the upstairs dining room. Specialities include rabbit, partridge, oxtail, lamb and *migas*: a kind of breadcrumbs flavoured with garlic.

❷ LA BODEGUILLA
Calle Dr Pulido, 2, Guadix; tel: 673-622 878; L and D; €
Old-style bodega (traditional wine bar) in the town centre with a great selection of regional wines. Popular with the locals for its excellent tapas.

Cubist architecture in Frigiliana

THE COSTA TROPICAL

The most attractive stretch of Spain's southern coast is the Costa Tropical (Tropical Coast), its name hinting at more exotic climes. That's where this route begins, before meandering through the enchanting hills of the Axarquia, behind the Costa del Sol.

DISTANCE: 96km (60 miles)
TIME: 1 day
START & END: Salobreña

There's a perfectly good motorway between the starting and the finishing points of this route. This is the slow alternative, using winding and climbing backroads. Take your time and enjoy the scenery.

THE RESORTS OF THE COSTA TROPICAL

Salobreña
Salobreña ❶ is the most attractive town on the Costa Tropical. Explore the old quarter on foot, a tight mass of whitewashed houses that swarm over an outcrop of rock set back from the beach. The remains of Moorish **castle** (daily 10am–2pm, 5.30–8.30pm in summer, 4–6pm in winter) stand

at the top of town; there are tremendous views from the battlements.

Begin the drive by taking the N340 west. This coastal road navigates the shoreline's many headlands; on the way you'll pass orchards of tropical fruits. Locally grown mangoes, avocados and bananas flourish in the microclimate and stock the shelves of the local shops and supermarkets.

Almuñécar and La Herradura
Almuñécar ❷ is an ancient town that the Romans knew as Sexi. Near the tourist information office, which is housed in a quaint mock Arab-style villa, is the

Almuñécar

Beachside El Peñón

Parque del Majuelo, where a small botanical garden of subtropical plants is laid out around the ruins of a Phoenecian-Roman fish-salting factory. A short stiff walk uphill is the half-restored **castle** that served as a holiday residence for the Nazrid kings of Granada.

A few more wiggles around the coast road lead to the much smaller resort of **La Herradura ❸**, which has an attractive beach between two headlands, Cerro Gordo and the Punta de la Mona. The latter is marked by a lighthouse. Beneath it is the pleasure boat harbour of Marina del Este, a departure point for scuba-diving trips.

Frigiliana

Leaving Granada behind, the N340 enters the province of Malaga. Bypass the vibrant family resort of **Nerja,** unless you want to make a stop at its beaches. From the outskirts of town, take the road inland to **Frigiliana ❹**. This is the prettiest and best-preserved town on the route, and strolling in its streets is a real delight.

THE AXARQUIA

Take the mountain road west from Frigiliana for Torrox, turning right on to the A7207 to climb towards Còmpeta. There is a mirador (viewpoint) just before you reach the town. **Còmpeta ❺** is the capital of the Axarquia region, characterised by whitewashed villages and isolated farmsteads climbing high

up its slopes. Stop for lunch at **Restaurante María ❶**.

Leave Cómpeta on the A7206 for Torre del Mar. A few kilometres downhill, turn right for **Archez** on the 'Ruta de Mudejar', named after the community of Muslims who stayed in Spain when the country was reconquered by the Christians. The 15th-century church tower of Archez was originally built as a minaret. Salares, the next village on, also has minaret, as well as a quaint Arab bridge.

From Archez, the scenic MA1111 takes you back towards the coast at **Vélez Málaga ❻**. If you need to cool down, make for the beach at Torre del Mar. Pick up the coastal motorway to return to Salobreña and enjoy a sunset meal at **El Peñón ❷**.

Looking over Almería city from the Alcazaba

THE DESERT AND ITS COAST

*Almería, Spain's southeastern province, is a region of stark desert landscapes
of undeniable grandeur. Low rainfall – and the consequent shortage of
water – has saved much of the east coast from over development.*

DISTANCE: 83km (52 miles)
TIME: 2 days
START & END: Almería city
POINTS TO NOTE: There are few places
to stop on this desert drive. Book into
a half-way hotel (see page 111), fill
up with fuel before you leave and carry
plenty of water – just in case.

Almería province is Mediterranean
Spain in the raw, a dry land governed
by the sun. The attractions here may
not at first be obvious, but they are surprisingly numerous, and the region conceals some spots of exquisite beauty.
This route is an introduction to Almería: a drive from the provincial capital through the desert, then down the
coast – passing some great beaches –
to take in the dramatic scenery around
the Cabo de Gata.

ALMERÍA THROUGH THE DESERT

There are only two major sights in the
city of **Almería ❶** to see before setting
out. One is Abd-er-Rahman III's massive **Alcazaba** (Tue–Sat 9am–6pm,
Sun 9am–3pm; free), which looms
large on the hilltop above the city.
Although an earthquake caused extensive damage in 1522, the crenellated
ochre walls and a section of the turreted ramparts stood firm, and now
provide wide-ranging vistas over the
city and the sea.

The second is the forbidding, fortified
Catedral (Mon–Sat 10am–6.30pm,
Sun 1.30–6.30pm). It was built in the
16th century, when Barbary pirates
were terrorising the coast.

If Almería gets little rain, it gets lots of
sunshine, claiming to have more hours
per annum (3,217 on average) than
any city in Europe. At night the city centre comes alive as bars and cafés take
over the narrow streets and alleys to the
northeast of the cathedral.

Tabernas

Leave the city heading north on the A92
motorway and turn off on to the N340
for **Tabernas ❷**, which stands in the
middle of Europe's only desert. The bad-

The Tabernas desert

lands and dry ravines were close enough to the archetypal deserts of North America to draw the Italian film-maker Sergio Leone here to shoot his 'spaghetti westerns' in the 1960s and 70s. Almería's 'Mini-Hollywood' has been used as a backdrop in innumerable films, and three of the former film sets can be visited. The largest is **Oasys** (www.oasys-parquetematico.com; tel: 902-533 532; mid-Apr–Oct daily 10am–6pm, later in summer, Nov–mid-Apr Sat–Sun 10am–6pm), to which a zoo, a cactus garden and swimming pool have been attached.

Sorbas

Continue on the N340 to **Sorbas** ❸, a town built above a gorge-cum-river meander and located near some very attractive karst limestone scenery. Further on, the N340 feeds into the motorway that runs the length of Spain's east coast; instead, continue on the minor road towards Mojácar.

DOWN THE EAST COAST

Mojácar

Mojácar ❹ is now synonymous with a beach resort, but the original town is a picturesque cluster of white cubic buildings, geographically and metaphorically raised above the excesses of the coast in the foothills of the Sierra de Cabrera.

There are good views from the old castle at the top of the town. A 16th-century chapel, La Ermita de los Dolores, built on the site of a mosque, serves as a souvenir shop. Everywhere in Mojácar you are likely to see the town's symbol, a figure called the Indalo, who is said to depict a prehistoric hunter holding a rainbow over his head. If you're hungry for lunch, there are several restaurants along the beach – try **Cabo Norte**, see ❶.

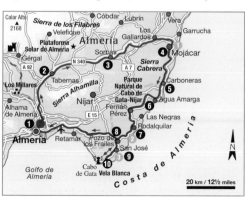

Carboneras

Take the scenic coast road, the AL5105, south from Mojácar to **Carboneras** ❺, a fishing village turned into a holiday resort. It is named after the old charcoal-burning industry which thrived here until all the available trees had been cut down. This curious town combines a magnificent broad sandy beach with

a cement works, desalination plant and power station.

Keep to the seafront through Carboneras and head for Agua Amarga (straight on past the power station). Shortly, on the left, you will see a sign for **Los Muertos** beach. A bumpy little road climbs to the lighthouse at **Mesa de Roldán**, from which there are good sea views. At this point you enter the Parque Natural del Cabo de Gata-Níjar, a nature and landscape reserve intended to protect the scenery and habitats from over development.

Agua Amarga

Back on the coast road you soon reach pleasant **Agua Amarga ❻**, a tiny seaside settlement that has preserved much of its charm. Its sandy beach is squeezed between two headlands. Park outside the town rather than negotiating the narrow streets. Agua Amarga makes a good overnight option; try **Mikasa** (see page 111).

Rodalquilar to Pozo de los Frailes

There is only one road out of Agua Amarga (other than the one you came in on), heading towards Almería city. Take this, but be ready to turn off on the first asphalted road to the left, signposted Fernán Pérez. At the T-junction turn left for San José (on the AL3106). After Las Hortichuelas, turn right for **Rodalquilar ❼** on the AL4200. It's worth dipping into

this village just to visit the information office for the nature reserve, but there's also a botanical garden, a geology museum and disused gold mines, which had been worked to the point of unprofitability by the end of the 1960s.

Resume the AL4200, still heading for San José. The next point of interest is the **Mirador de Amatista**, a viewing platform above the sea. Continue to **La Isleta del Moro,** a miniscule fishing village of small white houses built on an isthmus ending in a small island, or *isleta*. The restaurants here, naturally, specialise in fresh fish: take a seat on the terrace of **La Isleta del Moro ❷** and listen to the waves as you eat.

After Los Escullos, the road reaches another T-junction. Turn left, again for San José, and you find yourself in **Pozo de los Frailes ❽**. An ingenious Moorish well in the middle of the village demonstrates the importance given to managing water in the dry region of Almería: a donkey was used to rotate adjoined wheels to raise or lower water jars on a rope.

CABO DE GATA

San José

Drive into **San José ❾**, which is larger and more developed than some of the previous settlements, but still in proportion to its surroundings. There are some good places to

Agua Amarga

eat here, notably **Casa Miguel** ③, which serves up fresh seafood right in the middle of town.

Genoveses and Monsul

The Cabo de Gata proper, one of the Iberian Peninsula's few volcanic landscapes, is best approached from San José: turn off the roundabout and follow the brown signs for Genoveses and Monsul. This road turns into a dirt road (easily passable). Beyond a renovated windmill are two beautiful (and very popular) beaches on which development is prohibited. **Genoveses** is a curve of sand between two headlands; the next beach, **Monsul**, provided the setting for a scene in *Indiana Jones and the Last Crusade*.

Coastal walk to Vela Blanca

If you are in the mood for an easy walk, drive on until you can go no further. Park and continue on the track on foot – but do avoid the hottest part of the day, carry water and wear a sunhat as there's no shade. The path climbs around the headlands for two kilometres (1.2 miles), giving increasingly impressive sea views. When you get to the saddle beneath the **Vela Blanca** ⑩, an 18th-century watchtower, admire the vista before turning back.

Return to San José and follow the signs out of town for Almería on the AL3108 and turn left on the AL3201. This road meets the AL3115; turn right and continue to Almería.

Food and Drink

① CABO NORTE

Calle Piedra Villazar, 1 Mojacár Costa; tel: 950-473 119; www.restaurantecabonorte.es; L and D, closed Tue; €€

This unassuming hotel-restaurant serves the best food in town. The menu consists of creative versions of Spanish dishes, such as slow-cooked beef in sherry sauce and seafood salad with kiwi vinaigrette. There's a decent wine list too.

② LA ISLETA DEL MORO

Calle Mohamed Arráez, 28, La Isleta del Moro; tel: 950-389 713; www.pensionla isletadelmoro.com; L and D; €

The tables on the terrace of La Isleta del Moro could not be closer to the water's edge and the fish could not be fresher. Specialities on the menu include paella, fish stew and red prawns. On Sundays and in summer it is advisable to make a reservation.

③ CASA MIGUEL

Avda Correos, San José; tel: 950-380 027; http://casamiguelentierradecine.es; L, D and tapas; €€

The emphasis here is on local fish and seafood caught on the day. If you don't know what to order, ask for a *variado de pescado frito*: a selection of fried fish.

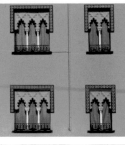

- ALBONDIGAS EN SALSA
  MEATBALLS IN WINESAUCE
- CROQUETAS DE QUESO MANCHEGO
  CHEESE CROQUETTES
- ESPINACAS CON GARBANZOS
  SPINACH WITH CHICKPEAS
- CARRILLERA IBERICA
  PORK MEAT (CHEEK) IN SAUCE
- CAMEMBERT CON FRAMBUES
  CAMEMBERT WITH RASPBERRY
- ROLLITOS DE BERENJENAS
  Y GAMBAS

DIRECTORY

Hand-picked hotels and restaurants to suit all budgets and tastes, organised by area, plus select nightlife listings, an alphabetical listing of practical information, a language guide and an overview of the best books and films to give you a flavour of the region.

Grand Alfonso XIII

ACCOMMODATION

Hotels are officially rated from one to five stars. The ratings, however, don't take into account charm, the quality of service or a friendly atmosphere. Small, family-run places in the lower categories can be more comfortable than large soulless establishments with gilded fittings and marble halls.

Hotel prices are posted at the reception desk and behind your room door. IVA (value added tax) is added on top. Most hotels have a low season and high season price. The latter may also apply during major fiestas.

Paradors (www.parador.es) are part of a state-run chain of prestigious hotels that either occupy historical monuments (monasteries, castles and the like) or are purpose-built in exceptional settings. Paradors offer a reliable standard of service, but often lack personality. Each parador has a restaurant specialising in regional cuisine.

At the other end of the scale, the cheapest option in a city is usually a backpacker's youth hostel; find cheap places to bunk at sites such as www.hostalworld.com.

Price for a double room in high season:
€ = below 75 euros
€€ = 75–125 euros
€€€ = 125–250 euros
€€€€ = above 250 euros

'Green tourism' has been booming in Spain in recent years and there are now a great many charming small rural hotels all over Andalucía. See www.rusticae.es.

There are also a great many self-catering village houses for rent – search for 'casa rural' or visit www.toprural.com. Owners of self-catering apartments and villas advertise on websites such as www.airbnb.com and www.ownersdirect.co.uk.

Camping and caravan sites are graded from one to three stars according to the facilities they provide. www.eurocampings.eu is a good place to start.

Seville

Alfonso XIII
Calle San Fernando, 2; tel: 954-917 000; www.hotel-alfonsoxiii-seville.com; €€€€
Expect old-style elegance in this renovated luxury hotel, built in neo-Mudéjar style in the 1920s around a splendid patio. Gastronomic and poolside restaurants.

Las Casas de la Judería
Plaza de Santa Maria de la Blanca; tel: 954-415 150; www.lascasasdelajuderiasevilla.com; €€€€
Twenty seven houses in the Santa Cruz quarter were restored and converted into this delightful boutique hotel with Moorish-inspired décor and rooms arranged around 30 inner courtyards. A

One of Las Casas de la Judería's 30 inner courtyards

restaurant, piano bar and small roof-top pool complete the picture.

La Casa del Maestro

Calle Niño Ricardo, 5; tel: 954-500 007; www.lacasadelmaestro.com; €€
The maestro in question is Manuel Serrapi Sánchez, one of Seville's most acclaimed guitarists, who was born nearby in 1904 and later made this his home. It is off the main tourist beat but very close to the Casa de Pilatos and a comfortable walk from Santa Cruz.

Hotel Zaida

Calle San Roque, 26; tel: 954-211 138; www.hotelzaida.com; €
This intimate budget hotel is in a delightful, restored 18th-century townhouse with an attractive Mudéjar-style courtyard and halls graced with Moorish arches.

Doñana National Park and Huelva

Doñana Blues

Sector el inglesillo, 129, Matalascañas; tel: 959-448 132; www.donanablues.com; €
Charming 15-room hotel surrounded by a verdant garden, near the beach and Doñana national park.

Hotel Toruño

Plaza del Acebuchal, 32, El Rocío; tel: 959-442 323; www.toruno.es; €€
A stand-alone balconied mansion near the church and wetlands. Of the 30 good rooms, one-third overlook the lake and there is a roof deck equipped with telescopes for star gazing and birdwatching.

Carmona and Osuna

Hotel Palacio Marqués de la Gomera

Calle San Pedro 20, Osuna; tel: 954-812 223; www.hotelpalaciodelmarques.es; €€
Smart boutique hotel in an 18th-century mansion with a gorgeous interior courtyard. The 20 rooms are bright, traditionally furnished and have lots of character.

Parador de Carmona

Alcázar, Carmona; tel: 954-141 010; www.parador.es; €€€€
Built around a 14th-century Arab fortress, this is one of the finest paradors in Spain. Bedrooms are plush, the dining hall is magnificent and there are spectacular views across the surrounding countryside.

Costa de la Luz

Argantonio

Calle Argantonio, 3, Cádiz; tel: 956-211 640; www.hotelargantonio.com; €€€
Stylish boutique hotel in a 19th-century building in the old town. The 15 rooms are decorated in Andalucían, French or colonial style and are equipped with large baths and flat-screen TVs. The hotel shop sells perfume and soaps by local artisans.

La Casa del Califa

Plaza de España, 16, Vejer de la Frontera; tel: 956-447 730; www.lacasadelcalifa.com; €€€

The Parador de Gibralfaro enjoys sea views

True to the Islamic heritage of Vejer, this atmospheric hotel in the centre is a maze of stone passageways leading to 18 rooms, individually designed with Moroccan furnishings and two suites with panoramic views. There are terraces and a flower-filled patio restaurant serving Arabian dishes.

Hostal Fenix
Calle Cazón, 7, Jerez de la Frontera; tel: 956-345 291; www.hostalfenix.com; €
A good budget option with white paint, bare bricks and dark wood, plus a small, pretty interior courtyard.

The White Towns

Hotel Enfrente Arte
Calle Real, 42, Ronda; tel: 952-879 088; www.enfrentearte.com; €€
Laid-back, funky hotel in an old house. Its facilities include a small pool, terraces with fine views, a library and Wii games. All drinks (wine, beer, juice) are included, as is the excellent buffet breakfast.

Parador de Arcos de la Frontera
Plaza del Cabildo, Arcos de la Frontera; tel: 956-700 500; www.parador.es; €€€€
The splendid views from this hotel, set on a cliff at the very top of the village, are worth a visit in their own right.

Parador de Ronda
Plaza de España, Ronda; tel: 952-877 500; www.parador.es; €€€€
Ronda's parador is famous for being spectacularly perched on the edge of the El Tajo gorge, and many of the rooms benefit from fabulous views. Book well in advance.

Gibraltar

The Rock Hotel
3 Europa Road; tel: +350-2007 3000; www.rockhotelgibraltar.com; €€€€
The Rock Hotel has been Gibraltar's landmark luxury hotel since it opened in 1932, entertaining celebrities including Sir Winston Churchill, Errol Flynn and John Lennon and Yoko Ono along the way. It has 84 guest rooms and suites with sea views.

Marbella

Marbella Club
Carretera N340, km 178; tel: 952-822 211; www.marbellaclub.com; €€€€
This classy 1950s hotel was the birthplace of the Marbella legend. Bungalow-style accommodation set among gardens which spread down to the beach. There is also a thalassotherapy spa.

Hotel Puente Romano
Bulevar Principe Alfonso von Hohenlohe; tel: 952-820 900; www.puenteromano.com; €€€€
A landmark on the 'Golden Mile' west of the town, this is a palatial hotel designed like a Moorish-Andalucían pueblo, with gardens and trickling fountains outside, and marble galore within. The nightclub, La Suite, is one of the best in town.

Marbella Club pool

The iconic Rock Hotel

Málaga

Hotel Domus
Calle Juan Valera, 20; tel: 952-297 164;
www.hoteldomus.es; €€
This lovely villa is just 15 minutes east of
the city centre in the attractive former fishing district of Pedregalejo, close to the best
city beaches. Fifteen ultra-modern rooms.

Dulces Dreams
Plaza de los Mártires, 6; tel: 951-357 869;
www.dulcesdreamshostel.com; €€
Budget boutique hotel that's a cut above
a youth hostel, although some of the eight
rooms do have shared bathrooms. Great
city-centre location, with bikes to rent.

Parador de Gibralfaro
Castillo de Gibralfaro; tel: 952-221 902;
www.parador.es; €€€€
This small, luxurious parador is spec-
tacularly situated next to the Castillo de
Gibralfaro, the Moorish fortress. Break-
fast comes with the best view in town.
Reservations essential.

Caminito del Rey

La Garganta
Barriada El Chorro; tel: 952-495 000;
www.3lagarganta.com; €€
Conveniently located at the end of the
Caminito del Rey, this hotel has a range
of rooms on offer.

Priego de Cordoba and Zuheros

Casa Olea
Calle Real, 2 Priego de Cordoba; tel: 957-
547 292; http://casaolea.com; €
Attractive hotel in a renovated 19th-cen-
tury building where the rooms are as you'd
expect: white walls, dark wood, stone
floors. The restaurant serves local specialities and there's a colourful interior patio.

Hotel Zuhayra
Calle Mirador, 10, Zuheros; tel: 957-694
693; www.zercahoteles.com; €
This is a simple but comfortable hotel,
with a good restaurant, situated in the
picturesque village of Zuheros.

Córdoba

Casa de los Azulejos
Calle Fernando Colón, 5; tel: 957-470 000;
www.casadelosazulejos.com; €€
This is an absolute delight: an elegant 17th-century house, whose name
derives from the wonderful coloured
tiles decorating its vaulted ceilings. The
style is a mix of Andalucían and Latin
American, and the eight pastel-coloured
rooms open on to a central patio.

Balcón de Córdoba
Calle Encarnación, 8; tel: 957-498 478;
www.balcondecordoba.com; €€€€
Stunning boutique hotel with 10 stylish,
contemporary rooms set around three
courtyards dotted with archaeological artefacts. The restaurant serves gourmet Anda-
lucian-Mediterranean dishes and there are
wonderful views from the roof terrace.

Hospedería Alma Andalusí
Calle Fernández Ruano, 5; tel: 626-901

Colonnaded courtyard of the Parador de Úbeda

656; www.almaandalusi.com; €
An ancient house in the Jewish quarter has been successfully transformed into a smart budget hotel with gleaming white walls, traditional tiled floors and contemporary furnishings.

Hotel Maestre
Calle Romero Barros, 4–6; tel: 957-472 410; www.hotelmaestre.com; €
Good-value hotel near the river. The rooms overlook an attractive inner courtyard. The management also runs a cheaper hostal down the street, as well as a small number of one- or two-bedroom apartments.

Jaén, Cazorla and Úbeda

Parador de Cazorla
Sierra de Cazorla; tel: 953-727 075; www.parador.es; €€€
In the heart of the sierra, this modern parador is an excellent base from which to explore Cazorla park.

Parador de Jaén
Castillo de Santa Catalina, Jaén; tel: 953-230 000; www.parador.es; €€€
One of the most impressive paradors in Spain, situated on a hill 4km (2.5 miles) west of the city, right next to Jaén's 8th-century Moorish castle and built in a similar style.

Parador de Úbeda
Plaza Vázquez Molina, Úbeda, 1; tel: 953-750 345; www.parador.es; €€€€
One of the oldest hotels in the parador chain, installed in a characterful 16th-century palace in the centre of Úbeda's old Renaissance quarter. Large and comfortable rooms. No pool.

Granada

Hotel Alhambra Palace
Plaza Arquitecto García de Paredes 1; tel: 958-221 468; www.h-alhambrapalace.es; €€€€
This may be a kitsch imitation of the Alhambra but it is still a nice place to stay, within walking distance of the real thing. Its magnificent terrace gives a superb view over the city and beyond.

Hostal Arteaga
Calle Arteaga, 3; tel: 958-208 841; www.hostalarteaga.co; €
Small, colourful en-suite rooms in a 19th-century building off the Gran Via de Colón.

Carmen de la Alcubilla del Caracol
Calle del Aire Alta, 12; tel: 958-215 551; www.alcubilladelcaracol.com; €€€
Seven antique-filled rooms painted in calming colours in a traditional carmen on the slopes of the Alhambra. Most have private terraces. Closed mid-July to Aug.

Casa Morisca
Cuesta de la Victoria, 9; tel: 958-221 100; www.hotelcasamorisca.com; €€€
Situated in the Albaicín, this is a tastefully converted 15th-century house with Moorish-inspired décor, a central courtyard and Alhambra views.

Inside the Hotel Alhambra Palace

Parador de Granada

Real de la Alhambra; tel: 958-221 440;
www.parador.es; €€€€

This prestigious hotel in a converted
15th-century monastery has an unbeatable view over the Alhambra. It gets
booked up well in advance for the prime
periods and it is essential to reserve at
all times.

The Alpujarras

Cuevas Pedro Antonio de Alarcón

Barriada San Torcuato, Guadix; tel: 958-664
986; www.cuevaspedroantonio.es; €€

The apartments of this unusual complex are caves carved out of the soft
rock, emulating the typical troglodyte
dwellings of the area; they sleep up to
eight people.

La Fragua

Calle San Antonio, 4, Trevélez; tel: 958-858
626; www.hotellafragua.com; €€

Comfortable hostal at the top of
Spain's highest village. A popular stop
for pony-trekking and hiking groups.
Outstanding views, a good restaurant
serving local cuisine and simple but
spotless rooms.

Las Terrazas de la Alpujarra

Plaza del Sol, 7, Bubión; tel: 958-763 034;
www.terrazasalpujarra.com; €

Simple but tasteful, and excellent value
for money. As well as a hostal, there are
apartments and a couple of small village houses. A favourite with trekkers
and bikers.

The Costa Tropical

Hotel Salambina

Carretera Málaga Km 326 Salobreña; tel:
958-612 949; http://hotelsalambina.com; €€

Superb views over the town, coast and
castle. The restaurant features local fish
and grilled meats on the menu.

Almería

Hotel Catedral

Plaza de la Catedral, 8, Almería; tel: 950-
278 178; www.hotelcatedral.net; €€€

This four-star boutique hotel in a grand
19th-century building is one of Almería's best. The 20 rooms are bright
and contemporary and food from the
gourmet restaurant is served in the
square outside.

Mikasa

Carretera Carboneras, Agua Amarga; tel:
950-138 073; www.mikasasuites.com; €€€

More like a private home than a hotel,
with artfully decorated rooms and
self-catering apartments. There is also
a pool, a spa – with five treatment
rooms, a dynamics poor and *hammam*
– and a beach bar.

El Mirador del Castillo

Mojácar Pueblo; tel: 694-454 768;
www.elmiradordelcastillo.com; €€

Open from March to October, this village house offers five traditionally furnished, tasteful rooms. There is a
café-bar (closes 11pm) plus a garden
with a pool. The place can be hired for
sole use.

Enrique Becerra dish

RESTAURANTS

Except in the remotest areas of the countryside, you are likely to be spoilt for choice for places to eat. They range from Michelin-starred restaurants to the local town bar, where presentation may be less glamorous but the food is likely to be just as good.

Places to eat in Andalucía can broadly be divided into the following categories: **Restaurantes** are usually open for lunch and dinner, and close during the afternoon and one day a week. A restaurant calling itself a *marisquería* specialises in shellfish and seafood, while an *asador* is the place for roast meats. *Venta, posada, mesón, casa de comidas* and *fonda* are all synonyms for restaurant, each with a slightly different connotation. A *venta* is a small, family-run restaurant serving down-to-earth country fare; well worth looking out for away from the coast. *Chiringuitos* are beachside restaurants that vary in size, quality and level of formality. In and around markets is a good place to look for cheap, traditional restaurants where the locals go. A restaurant will always offer a *menú del día* at lunchtime on weekdays – much cheaper than ordering à la carte. You will need to reserve a table in a formal restaurant at a busy time but otherwise you can just turn up.

Bars. You can generally eat in any bar anywhere, even if it is only a round of cold tapas. Most bars will serve you toast or pastries for breakfast and willingly make you a sandwich (*bocadillo*) to your specifications at any time. Many bars also double as restaurants, serving both tapas and full meals in a *comedor* (dining room).

Cafeterías are middle-range establishments, more common in cities, that are generally more comfortable than bars. Like bars, they usually serve snacks and meals.

Seville

La Azotea
Calle Jesús del Gran Poder, 31; tel: 955-116 748; www.laazoteasevilla.com; €€
Highly regarded restaurant serving upmarket contemporary tapas, making the most of the wonderful local produce.

Bodeguita Casablanca
Calle Adolfo Rodríguez, 12; tel: 954-224 114; www.bodeguitacasablanca.com; €€
Convenient bodega opposite the Archivo de Indias, decorated with bullfighting memorabilia. Serves traditional Spanish cuisine, including Andalucían tripe (*callos*); the house speciality is stew.

Prices for three-course meal per person with a half-bottle of house wine:
€ = under €20
€€ = €20–€10
€€€ = €40–€60
€€€€ = over €60

Casa Balbino

Egaña–Oriza

Calle San Fernando, 41; tel: 954-227 254; www.restauranteoriza.com; €€€

The Basque-inspired cuisine of this elegant, modern restaurant near the Murillo gardens is among the best in Andalucía. Reservations recommended.

Enrique Becerra

Calle Gamazo, 2; tel: 954-213 049; www.enriquebecerra.com; €€

Small restaurant in an old Seville house in the El Arenal area. Serves high-quality Andalucían fare and has a popular bar as well, where the tapas are a gourmet cut above the rest. It's on its way to making 100% of its dishes gluten-free.

Espacio Eslava

Calle Eslava, 3; tel: 954-906 568; www.espacioeslava.com; €€

Fashionable restaurant and tapas bar in the San Lorenzo district. Dishes are traditional with a contemporary twist. The ingredients are local and seasonal; they grow their own organic vegetables.

Hosteria del Laurel

Plaza de los Venerables, 5; tel: 954-220 295; http://hosteriadellaurel.com; €€

The fictional character of Don Juan was supposedly invented in this house, now a highly rated restaurant. You can have tapas at the bar or a full meal at an outdoor table in the picturesque square.

Antequera

Caserio de San Benito

Carretera Málaga–Córdoba, km 87, exit 86 Antequera; tel: 952-111 103; www.caseriodesanbenito.com; €€

Traditional country-house restaurant specialising in 'recovering grandmother's homemade recipes': grilled meats, lamb chops, rice with rabbit and Antequera's thick chilled tomato soup, *porra*. Good wine list.

Costa de la Luz

El Balandro

Alameda de Apodaca, 22, Cádiz; tel: 956-220 992; www.restaurantebalandro.com; €€

Understated but smart, this is a formal restaurant with three dining rooms, a long bar serving tapas and windows overlooking the bay. The menu is wide ranging, with superb *jamón ibérico* and an extensive wine and sherry list.

La Carbona

Calle San Francisco de Paula, 2, Jerez de la Frontera; tel: 956-347 475; www.lacarbona.com; €€€

Very spacious, sociable dining room under the cavernous vaulted ceilings and arches of a converted sherry bodega. Specials include swordfish or prawns *a la plancha*, cooked on the grill in an open kitchen. Good selection of wine and sherry.

Casa Balbino

Plaza del Cabildo, 11, Sanlúcar de Barrameda; tel: 956-360 513; www.casabalbino.es; €€

Al-fresco dining at De Locos Tapas

At the heart of old Sanlúcar, this renowned and popular bar/restaurant is a long-standing family-run business. Locals and visitors sit on barrels and at tables in the square to feast on an extensive choice of seafood, including lobster.

Casa Bigote

Calle Bajo de Guia, 10, Sanlúcar de Barrameda; tel: 956-362 696; www.restaurantecasabigote.com; €€€
One of the famed seafood establishments in Bajo de Guia, with a choice of tapas and more substantial fare. The paella is particularly good.

El Jardín del Califa

Plaza de España, 16, Vejer de la Frontera; tel: 956-451 706; www.califavejer.com; €€
For a sense of Vejer's Moorish past, Arabic dishes (including cous cous and lamb tagine with almonds and plums) are served in an enclosed and pleasant patio garden with Moroccan decor. Reservations recommended.

Juanito

Calle Pescadería Vieja, 8–10, Jerez de la Frontera; tel: 956-334 838; www.barjuanito.com; €
Thriving local tapas bar in Jerez old town. A long list of *raciones* includes vermicelli with prawns, artichokes and excellent manchego.

Misiana

Calle Sancho IV El Bravo, Tarifa; tel: 956-627 083; www.misiana.com; €€

Appealing to Tarifa's fashionable crowd, this is a smart, modern lounge bar near the town centre, with a cosmopolitan array of tapas and cocktails.

Posada La Sacristia

Calle San Donato, 8, Tarifa; tel: 956-681 759; www.lasacristia.net; €€€
Posada La Sacristia has been designed to make good use of the arches and corners of a brick courtyard at the heart of a 17th-century building. The menu is a contemporary mix of Moroccan and Andalucían.

Romerijo

Calle Ribera del Marisco, 1, El Puerto de Santa Maria; tel: 902-541 254; www.romerijo.com; €€
An informal seafood eatery on the riverfront, Romerijo is very popular with locals. Good value fresh catch, steamed or fried and priced by the kilogram.

The White Towns

Albacara

Calle Tenorio, Ronda; tel: 952-873 855; www.hotelmontelirio.com; €€€
Comfortable, traditionally styled restaurant in a hotel: occupying a historic house and with its own Turkish bath. Good-quality regional and international dishes are served, notably roast lamb and suckling pig cooked the traditional way.

Casa Santa Pola

Cuesta de Santo Domingo, 3, Ronda; tel: 952-879 208; www.rsantapola.com; €€€
Housed in a pretty mansion built over a

El Jardín del Califa

9th-century mosque next to the Puente Nuevo. Magnificent terrace views. The menu features creative interpretations of Andalucían cuisine.

De Locos Tapas

Arquitecto Pons Sorolla, 7, Ronda; tel: 951-083 772; www.de-locos-tapas.com; €
Excellent local and international tapas, with a regularly changing menu. Generous portions. Reservations recommended as there are only a few tables.

Mesón de la Molinera

Urbanization El Santiscal, Avenida Sombrero de Tres Picos, 17, Arcos de la Frontera; tel: 956-708 002; www.4mesondelamolinera.com; €€
The elegant restaurant in this fine hotel, which occupies an old oil mill, serves Andalucían cuisine using fresh local produce; there are local wines on the menu too. On the banks of a lake with lovely views of the town.

Málaga

Astorga

Calle Gerona, 11; tel: 952-342 563; www.mesonastorga.com; €€€
The food has earned this lively, friendly restaurant the reputation of being one of the city's best, and reservations are essential. The emphasis is on seafood, notably fresh prawns, octopus, anchovies and scallops.

El Calafate

Calle Andres Pérez 6; tel: 952-229 344; €
This vegetarian restaurant serves good-value, copious dishes. Even if you are not a vegetarian, the light food can be a welcome respite from all the meat and fish that dominates Andalucían menus. There are vegan options as well.

José Carlos García

Plaza de la Capilla, Puerto de Málaga; tel: 952-003 588; www.restaurantejcg.com; €€€€
The restaurant of José Carlos García, one of Spain's top chefs, serves imaginative dishes. The *menu de degustación* is a good way to sample the house specialities. Reservations essential.

El Mesón de Cervantes

Calle Alamos 11; tel: 952-216 274; www.elmesondecervantes.com; €
One of the best tapas bars in town with vegetarian options such as goat's-cheese quiche and mushroom risotto. There's a good selection of wine including some local varieties.

Córdoba

Bodegas Campos

Calle Lineros, 32; tel: 957-497 500; www.bodegascampos.com; €€€
Colourful, award-winning restaurant in a former wine cellar that has attracted a number of VIP diners over the years. It serves variations on classical Córdoba cuisine. The cinnamon ice cream is particularly good.

El Caballo Rojo

Calle Cardenal Herrero, 28; tel: 957-475

Leafy Taberna Salinas

375; www.elcaballorojo.com; €€€
Long-established restaurant in a street behind the Mosque. The menu includes Moorish dishes based on medieval recipes. Reservations essential.

Cuatromanos

Calle San Felipe, 13; tel: 957-110 591; www.cuatromanos.es; €€€
Run by two brothers (*cuatro manos* = four hands), this contemporary restaurant near Plaza de las Tendillas specialises in contemporary Andalucían cuisine enhanced with international flavours. They also serve tapas.

ReComiendo

Calle Alcala Zamora, 5; tel: 957-107 351; www.recomiendopower.com; €€€
Andalucían Nouvelle Cuisine is on the menu at this unassuming restaurant in the northeast of the city. There's a new tasting menu each month featuring chef Periko Ortega's creative use of local products, inspired by local life.

Taberna Salinas

Calle Tundidores, 3; tel: 957-482 950; www.tabernasalinas.com; €€
One of Córdoba's oldest places to eat, this taberna has been operating since 1879 and also has a bodega and a pretty patio. The place to try black pudding and other local specialities.

Jaen

Horno de Salvador

Subida del Castillo de Santa Catalina; tel:
953-230 528; http://hornodesalvador.com; €€€
One of Jaén's best restaurants. It's address is merely 'the road up to the castle' – that's how easy it is to find. If you are not sure what to order, ask for the sampler menu, the *menú de degustación*: not cheap but it keeps the final bill under control.

Taberna Casa Gorrión

Calle Arco de Consuelo 7, Jaén; tel: 953-232 000; http://Tabernagorrion.es; €
The oldest bar in the city, founded in 1888 (Gorrión – "sparrow" – was the nickname of the founder), and still drawing a crowd of faithful regulars. Two staple ingredients of the dishes on the menu are cured manchego cheese and *bacalao* (salt cod).

Taberna La Manchega

Calle Bernardo López, 8 Jaén; tel: 953-232 192; €
Authentic bar and restaurant in one of the backstreets of the city. Don't expect sophisticated décor. This is an authentic bar and what you can rely on are the excellent tapas and daily specials.

Granada

Chikito

Plaza del Campillo, 9; tel: 958-223 364; www.restaurantechikito.com; €€€
This long-established restaurant (the poet Lorca was a regular) is one of the best eateries in the region. Chef Antonio

Casa Puga

Torres serves consistently good regional dishes such as *rabo de toro* (braised oxtail) and *bacalao* (baked cod) along with more innovative fare. It's best to reserve, especially at weekends.

Cunini
Plaza Pescadería, 14; tel: 958-267 587; www.marisqueriacunini.com; €€€
This friendly restaurant close to the cathedral is the best place for fresh fish and seafood in Granada. It has a tent-like terrace for outdoor dining in summer.

Hicuri Art Vegan
Plaza de los Girones, 4; tel: 958-987 473; www.restaurantehicuriartvegan.com; €
This vegan restaurant in Realejo has a good choice of dishes as well as smoothies, juices and herbal teas.

Rincón de Lorca
Calle Angulo, 3; tel: 958-536 732; www.restauranterincondelorca.es; €€€
Located in the Hotel Reina Cristina in the heart of town, this is one of Granada's most reliable restaurants, serving regional dishes prepared with a modern touch.

Terraza las Tomasas
Carril de San Augustín, 4; tel: 958-224 108; www.lastomasas.com; €€€
The regional cuisine is almost as good as the superb view over the Alhambra. Good cocktails. Reservations recommended.

El Trillo
Callejon Aljibe del Trillo, 3; tel: 958-225 182; www.restaurante-eltrillo.com; €€€
Delightful and very well-respected restaurant in the heart of the Albaicín. Specialises in authentic Spanish cuisine, with a particularly strong Basque presence on the menu.

Costa Tropical

Pesetas
Calle Bóveda, 11, Salobreña; tel: 958-610 182; www.restaurante-pesetas.es; €€
As well as good food (mainly fish), this restaurant offers an incomparable view from its rooftop terrace; a great place to come and cool off on a summer's evening.

Almería

Casa Puga
Jovellanos 7; tel: 950-231 530; http://barcasapuga.es; €
A traditional bodega – with hams hanging from the ceiling and marble-topped tables and walls covered with *azulejos* – in the historical part of the city centre that has been going since 1870. Try a glass of the local Albuñol wine with your food. Closed Sun.

El Quinto Toro
Calle Reyes Católicos, 6; tel: 950-239 135; €
Top-notch atmospheric tapas bar taking its name from the fifth bull in the *corrida* (always reputed to be the best). Friendly service and mouthwatering mains.

Live music at Tablao El Cardenal

NIGHTLIFE

Spaniards are enormously social, and you'll find nightlife even in the smaller cities. But you'll find most to do in the bigger cities, and Seville stands out as the best. In summer, there is always a lot happening on the Costa del Sol.

There are broadly two kinds of bar in Spain: one for daytime clientele, offering food but no atmosphere; the other open in the evening or night. The latter only serves drinks and its reputation depends on its ambience and the music it plays.

Nightlife is therefore in two shifts. If you are thinking of going to bed before breakfast, the *tapeo* is for you: a tour around the local tapas bars terminating around 11pm. Only after this time do serious partygoers set out for the night, starting in a *bar de copas* – a bar with atmosphere but probably few chairs and no food at all. After midnight, the dance clubs open and a good night out goes on until at least 6am. Either kind of night out can be combined with a play, show or concert – most cities put on a busy programme of artistic events.

The best nights out are during the main fiestas of Andalucía: Cadiz's carnival, Seville's April Fair and other extended periods of revelry.

Córdoba

Café Málaga
Calle Málaga, 3; tel: 957-476 298;
www.facebook.com/cafemalagalivemusic

This bar, popular among those in the know, is situated a few minutes' north of the Mezquita and has a great atmosphere. It puts on a busy programme of live jazz by up-and-coming performers and also some cabaret. It is open from 4pm to 3am.

Gran Teatro
Calle Gran Capitán, 3; tel: 957-480 644;
https://teatrocordoba.es
City orchestra recitals and various music and theatre performances in a proud, old, horseshoe-shaped hall. The Gran Teatro also coordinates the Córdoba Guitar Festival each year in July

Tablao El Cardenal
Calle Buen Pastor, 2; tel: 691-217 922;
www.tablaocardenal.es
An 18th-century aristocratic house transformed to become a *tablao* (flamenco venue). There is a show every night from Monday to Saturday at 8.15 or 9pm. It consists of song, dance and guitar, involves seven performers and lasts about one and a half hours. Tickets are available online.

Costa de la Luz

Café Teatro Pay Pay
Calle Silencio, Barrio del Populo, Cádiz; tel:
956-252 543; www.cafeteatropaypay.com
This popular café in the centre of Cádiz manages to be a fully equipped cultural centre. There is always something going

on, be it cabaret, book launches, conjuring acts, exhibitions, conferences or theatre. If you don't understand Spanish you'll probably appreciate the concerts of jazz, pop, blues or the performances by flamenco dancers or magicians. Wednesday is open night for singer-songwriters.

La Quilla

Antonio Burgos, Playa de la Caleta, Cádiz; tel: 956-226 466; http://quilla.es

A versatile place with an impressive view of the castle and the sea from its terrace, which is good at any time of the day: breakfast (classical music and homemade cakes, fresh juice, and newspapers), tapas, lunch, afternoon coffee, dinner and finally cocktails in the evening. In the winter there is a fireplace indoors.

La Taberna Flamenca

Angostillo de Santiago, 3, Jerez de la Frontera; tel: 956-323 693; www.latabernaflamenca.com

A restaurant occupying a former wine cellar. In winter there are shows Tuesday to Saturday at 10.30pm. In summer there is also a show at 2.30pm on Tuesdays, Wednesdays and Saturdays. The performance lasts about 50 minutes. You can either pay for a meal and the show or just a drink and the show.

Granada and the Costa Tropical

Camborio

Camino de Sacromonte, 47, Granada; tel: 958-221 215; https://www.facebook.com/ElCamborioGR/

A renowned bar and discotheque in Sacromonte with a variety of dance floors and spaces, including a patio and caves. It takes around 20 minutes to get there from Plaza Nueva on foot but there is a bus until 2am. Don't arrive before midnight.

Eshavira Club

Postigo de la Cuna, 2, Granada; http://eshaviraclub.wordpress.com

A dimly lit bar which puts on performances of live jazz and sultry flamenco – here you can be sure of seeing the real thing, not the package presented to tourists. It is a little way out of the centre, off Calle Elvira.

Granada 10

Cárcel Baja, 10, Granada; tel: 958-256 997

An old cinema in the city centre (near the Gran Via colon) that has been converted into a dance club, keeping much of the beautiful original décor. It has a faithful clientele who keep it busy. Opens at 12.30am. Wednesday is hip-hop/funk/house night.

Sunem Playa

Paseo Maritime, 2, Salobreña; tel: 958-828 807; https://www.facebook.com/SunemPlayaOficial/

There's not a great choice of nightlife on the Costa Tropical, but this is at least a bar with some life to it. Sunem Playa enjoys a beautiful location at the head of the beach beside Salobreñas emblematic pennon. It organises theme

Spanish soprano Ainhoa Arteta dazzles at the Nerja Caves

nights, fiestas and evenings of monologues and humour that will test your Spanish while you enjoy your drink.

Zambra María la Canastera
Camino del Sacromonte, 89, Granada; tel: 958-121 183; www.marialacanastera.com
This cave-venue is highly renowned for its flamenco shows and has been visited by the king of Spain. You need to buy a combined ticket for dinner and the performance.

Baeza
Café Teatro Central
Calle Obispo Narváez, 19; tel: 953-744 355; https://www.facebook.com/CafeTeatroCentral/
This is a beautiful bar in its own right, occupying a 19th-century mansion southeast of Plaza de España. It is filled with quirky and kitsch objets d'art and has a fountain. Even better, there's usually live music on Thursday, Friday and Saturday nights.

Málaga, Marbella and the Costa del Sol
Casino Marbella
Hotel H10 Andalucía Plaza, Puerto Banús; tel: 952-814 000; www.casinomarbella.com
Gambling is a national pastime in Spain, and Andalucía's casinos are elegant night-time venues, offering the full gamet of American and French roulette, black jack and other traditional casino games. The restaurant here is open until 2am.

Flamenco Ana Maria
Plaza Santo Cristo, 4, Marbella; tel: 667-384 946; hardoklaamann.wixsite.com/flamencomarbella
Small flamenco venue in the old town of Marbella. Phone after 4pm to reserve a place. The show starts at 10.30pm. Closed Mondays.

Kelipé Centro D'Arte Flamenco
Calle Muro de Puerta Nueva, 10, Málaga; tel: 665-097 359; http://www.kelipe.net
Head here for an authentic evening of flamenco, run by a family of artists. Shows are held on Thursdays, Fridays and Saturdays (9–11pm). The ticket price includes two drinks.

Lineker's Bar
Muelle De Ribera, Puerto Banús; tel: 952-810 918; www.linekersgroup.com
It describes itself as 'world famous', but others considered Lineker's infamous. Popular with stag and hen parties, it is not a place for a quiet drink. Twenty-five screens relay major international sports events. Various activities are organised to order: for instance, you can learn to make cocktails as well as drink them.

Nerja Caves
Carretera de Maro, Nerja; tel: 952-529 520; www.cuevadenerja.es
One of the most remarkable venues is the Nerja Cave system, which holds ballet, music and theatre performances during the summer months.

Olivia Valere
Caretera de Istán 0.8km, Marbella;

Performance at the Teatro de la Maestranza

www.oliviavalere.com
Often described as the most famous nightclub on the Costa del Sol. It charges a hefty entrance fee but that's the price to bop alongside visiting celebs and the local glitterati.

Tablao los Amayas

Calle Beatas 21, Málaga; tel: 686-936 804; www.flamencomalagacentro.com
Two flamenco shows lasting an hour and ten minutes at 7 and 9pm include a singer, a guitarist and three dancers. The admission includes a drink.

Seville

La Carbonería

Levies, 18; tel: 954-214 460
A former coal store has been converted into a renowned venue for flamenco music and dance. It attracts hordes of tourists but still preserves a sense of authenticity. Don't go if you are just mildly curious and want background entertainment. Here, you are expected to take it seriously and appreciate the art you are being offered. Open 10am–3pm.

Doña Maria Hotel

Calle Don Remondo, 19; tel: 954-224 990; www.hdmaria.com
The terrace bar of this hotel is a popular place to go for drinks in the evening, either after a hard day's sightseeing or in preparation for a night out. Its big draw is its unbeatable view of the floodlit Giralda.

Los Gallos

Plaza de Santa Cruz, 11; tel: 954-216 981; www.tablaolosgallos.com
This *tablao flamenco* is one of the legendary venues of Seville in which to see the traditional music and dance of Andalucía. It has been operating since 1966. There are two performances a night, at 8.30pm and 10.30pm, each featuring five performers and lasting an hour and a half. The aim is to show the visitor a variety of '*palos flamencos*' (styles of singing).

Puerto de Cuba

Calle Betis, Triana; tel: 697-300 355; www.puertodecubasevilla.com
There are a number of good places to go for a quiet night out with friends on Calle Betis in Triana, just across the river from the centre. This bar is next to Puente de San Telmo, looking across the water at the Torre del Oro. It consists of a broad terrace by the river spread with comfortable chairs and an atmosphere created by good lighting and carefully selected music. A place to relax.

Teatro de la Maestranza

Plaza de Colón, s/n; tel: 954-223 344; www.teatrodelamaestranza.es
Serville's opera house was designated as one of the main cultural venues for Seville's Expo '92. The building seats 1,800 and puts on a varied programme of opera, orchestra recitals and soloists, classical ballet, modern dance and flamenco music.

Centre Pompidou Málaga

A–Z

A

Addresses

Most streets in Spain are denominated 'calle' but often this word is omitted in addresses. The number comes after the name. The abbreviation 's/n' (*sin número*/without number) means the address has no street number and is easy to find.

Age restrictions

The legal minimum age for buying or drinking alcohol, or for driving a car, is 18. The age of consent is 16.

B

Budgeting

A beer or glass of house wine may cost as little as one euro in a neighbourhood bar; expect to pay €2–6 anywhere else.

A lunchtime set menu in a mid-range restaurant will be €10–15 per person, but a meal from the full menu will cost €20–30. In a top-class restaurant you can normally expect to pay €60–90.

Accommodation will likely cost €60–70 per night for a double room in a rural guesthouse, €80–120 in a pleasant small boutique hotel in a city and anything over €200 in upmarket hotels. Anywhere near the coast prices are higher in July and August, and cities are more expensive during special events such as fiestas.

A single bus ticket in a city should cost €1.50–2. Taxis are metered, with higher fares at night.

Admission to museums and sights costs from around €5 in small centres to €12–15 in major museums, with reductions for anyone aged under 18 or over 65.

C

Children

Andalucíans adore children and Spain is a very child-friendly place. Children go out with their parents even late at night: babysitters are practically unheard of (although available for tourists at larger hotels). Although you won't find facilities for children everywhere, you will almost always find obliging people to provide you with what you want (restaurant staff will cater to particular culinary requirements etc). Modern tourist-orientated restaurants have play areas and high chairs, but elsewhere you will need to provide your own folding seat. Baby-changing areas are fairly infrequent except in motorway service areas.

Very few hotels are adults only, and family rooms are commonly available; some hotels will allow children to stay in their parents' room at no extra charge. Every monument has a reduced tariff for a child (or free admission). Young

children travel free on public transport; older children at a concessionary rate.

Clothing

Although Andalucíans like to dress elegantly, they do not demand the same of visitors. Informal dress is acceptable almost everywhere, although avoid anything too garish or too scanty when visiting cathedrals and religious sites, and men should not go bare-chested anywhere but the beach or poolside. Light clothing is adequate for much of the year on the coast, with a light sweater or jacket for the occasional cool evening. In winter take a heavy sweater or fleece and raincoat or umbrella. More formal clothing (jacket and tie for men) is usual in casinos and more elegant dining spots.

Crime and safety

Andalucía is as safe as most places in Western Europe and if you take sensible precautions you should have no trouble. Nevertheless, as a disorientated tourist you may be a target for opportunistic thieves. In busy tourist areas watch out for pickpockets who sometimes work in pairs: while one person distracts you, the other dips into your bag. Lock valuables in a hotel safety deposit box and never take them to the beach. Keep a copy of your passport (separately). Don't leave anything visible in your car. Wear a bag that straps across you.

Occasionally, on motorways you may see a motorist apparently in difficulty, or who indicates that you have a problem with your car and insists that you pull over on the hard shoulder. This is often a trick: take great care who you stop for.

Be very careful with fire in the countryside. Spain has a serious problem with forest fires in the summer months. A carelessly discarded match or cigarette butt can set off a blaze that quickly becomes out of control.

Customs

Within reason and subject to the judgement of customs officials, EU nationals are not restricted in what they can bring into Spain or take back to their own countries of origin, as long as it is for personal use. Guidelines are available giving recommended amounts of tobacco and alcohol. Note that the rules for Britain will probably change once it leaves the European Union: check with HM Revenue & Customs before you travel. If you are bringing more than €1,000 in cash into Spain it must be declared. Non-EU citizens can reclaim the VAT paid on items bought in Spain as they leave the country.

Disabled travellers

Spain is making rapid strides in its services for people with disabilities, in line with EU standards, but you may still encounter problems. Few restaurants specifically cater for people in wheelchairs. The staff may have a ramp to cope with entrance steps but it is rare to find a toilet adapted for disabled people.

However, the Spanish are generally accommodating and it is likely that restaurant staff will help lift your wheelchair in and shuffle tables round to make you comfortable.

Tourist offices will provide details of wheelchair-friendly hotels, beaches, monuments and restaurants, but it is wise to call in advance if you have special requirements. Most city buses are adapted for wheelchairs, and you can request a taxi specifically intended for wheelchair users.

The Spanish tourism website, spain. info, devotes a section to Accessible Tourism, with advice on fully equipped restaurants, accommodation, transport and sights and activities.

E

Electricity

The electricity supply in Spain is 220 volts AC, 50 Hertz. Spanish plugs have two round pins. Travel adapters are available in department stores and hypermarkets, but you should check that your appliance will work at this voltage.

Embassies and consulates

Australia: Torre Espacio, Paseo de la Castellana, 259D, Madrid; tel: 913-536 600; www.spain.embassy.gov.au.

Canada: Torre Espacio, Paseo de la Castellana, 259D, Madrid; tel: 913-828 400; www.canadainternational.gc.ca/spain-espagne.

Ireland: Paseo de la Castellana, 46; tel: 914-364 093; www.embassyofireland. es. There are Honorary Consulates in Seville and Malaga.

UK: Torre Espacio, Paseo de la Castellana, 259D; tel: 917-146 300; http://ukinspain.fco.gov.uk. There is also a consulate in Malaga.

US: Calle Serrano 75; tel: 915-872 200; http://es.usembassy.gov.

Emergencies

In the event of an emergency, call 112 to be directed to the service (ambulance, fire brigade, police) you require. You will be attended to by someone who speaks English.

Alternatively, call the service you require directly:

National police: 091
Municipal police: 092
Fire brigade: 080
Ambulance: 061

Etiquette

Spanish people set great store on human contact and common courtesy. Always say hello when entering a place where there are people (even a lift) and goodbye when you leave. '*Gracias*' (thank you) is used less frequently than in English but always appreciated. Spanish people can seem animated when they speak and their language makes great use of the imperative – but don't take this for hostility. Speaking a little Spanish will endear you to the locals and, if you can, remember

Taking in the sights from a tour bus

to use the formal '*usted*' and not familiar '*tu*' form when addressing someone you don't know – although allowances will be made for you if you sound over friendly. In bars and restaurants, paying the bill is considered the privilege of the host, so don't insist too much on going halves unless you know the person well.

Fiestas and festivals

Andalucía has a prodigious programme of traditional and arts festivals throughout the year. The best include:

February: Carnival, the best being in Cádiz

March/April: Easter Week processions in Seville and other cities

April: April Fair in Seville

May: Jerez de la Frontera horse fair; Patios Festival in Córdoba; El Rocio pilgrimage

June: St John's Night (bonfires in many places); Gypsy pilgrimage in Cabra

June/July: International Festival of Music and Dance, Granada

July: Virgen del Carmen – patron saint of fishing communities – celebrated on the coast with parades of decorated boats

August: Exaltación del Río Guadalquivir in Sanlúcar de Barrameda

September: Fair in Ronda including bullfight in period costume

September/October: Grape harvest festivals, especially in Jerez de la Frontera

G

Guides and tours

English-speaking guides can be hired through local tourist offices (see page 131). Guided tours and excursions can be booked at most hotels or through any of the numerous travel agencies (*agencia de viaje*). **Insight Guides** (www.insightguides.com/holidays) offers holidays to numerous destinations around the globe, including Andalucía. You can book trips, transfers and a range of exciting experiences through our local experts, taking in the highlights of the region.

H

Health

Before you travel

You don't need inoculations to visit Spain and there are no particular health issues to be aware of.

Public health services are generally of a high standard, although it is advisable to take out travel insurance in case you need more than basic medical treatment. EU nationals are entitled to free basic healthcare at state clinics or hospitals with an EHIC card, and most treatments are free. Private medical attention, of course, is not covered by this scheme. EU provisions may not apply to British citizens after March 2019.

If you need prescription drugs it is best to bring them with you. Spanish

Pottery and baskets make good souvenirs

medication may differ from your own and chemists in Spain do not honour foreign prescriptions. Make a note of the generic name of your medicine in case you need to find extra supplies locally.

Medical facilities

Most hospitals (*hospitales*) have an emergency department (*urgencias*), and there are also smaller health centres (*centro sanitario*, *centro de asistencia primaria*, *CAP* or similar) in many towns and districts that can provide immediate assistance. There are also many private clinics and doctors, which hotels will be able to recommend; consulates also keep lists of English-speaking doctors.

For minor complaints, look for a *farmacia* (pharmacy) identified by a big sign with a flashing green cross. They are open Mon–Fri 9.30am–1.30pm and 5–8pm, Sat 9am–1.30pm, and outside these hours local duty rotas operate. Spanish pharmacists are trained and knowledgeable and can advise you on minor ailments. Lists of current duty pharmacies or *farmacias de guardia* are posted in all pharmacy windows, local newspapers, and, often, in tourist offices.

Note that dentistry, which can be expensive, may not be fully covered under your insurance policy and you may have to put up with temporary treatment and sort the problem out when you get home.

Sensible precautions

The summer sun can be a potential hazard in the outdoors, whether you are on the beach or walking in the hills. Beware of sunburn, heat-stroke and dehydration. Wear a hat, use sunscreen and choose shade when you can.

Spanish tap water is generally safe, although many people prefer to drink bottled water. Drinking from streams, no matter how clear they appear to be, is a risky business. If you are going hiking, plan to carry water. Iodine tablets are the best water-purifying tablets presently on the market, but they are still not 100 percent guaranteed.

At mealtimes, take it easy until your body has become accustomed to changes in climate and diet. Beware of excessive alcohol consumption. It can have devastating effects on your stomach, especially when eating food fried in olive oil with liberal doses of garlic and peppers. You are particularly warned to partake sparingly of cheap wine, as this is almost certain to give you a headache or worse, and is foolish in a country where superb wines can be enjoyed for just a little more.

Hours and holidays

Shops and offices generally open Mon–Sat 9am–1pm and 4pm–8pm. Large supermarkets, out-of-town stores and shops in coastal resorts generally do not close for a lunch break. Most small shops close on Sunday, but you will always find somewhere open – even

Many of Andalucía's cities have thriving LGBTQ scenes

if it's only a petrol station. Banks follow shop opening hours but are often closed on Saturday afternoon and certainly on Sunday.

The public holidays celebrated across Andalucía are:

January 1 New Year's Day (Año Nuevo)
January 6 Twelfth Night (Día de los Reyes)
February 28 Andalucía Day (Día de Andalucía)
Holy Thursday (Jueves Santo), moveable feast, March or April
Good Friday (Viernes Santo), moveable feast, March or April
May 1 Labour Day (Fiesta del Trabajo)
August 15 Assumption of the Virgin (Fiesta de la Asunción)
October 12 Columbus Day (Día de la Hispanidad)
November 1 All Saints' Day (Todos los Santos)
December 6 Constitution Day (Día de la Constitución)
December 8 Immaculate Conception (Inmaculada Concepción)
December 25 Christmas Day (Navidad)
  Each town or city has two extra holidays of its own.

I

Insurance

The most comprehensive travel insurance should cover trip cancellation, delay, medical expenses – naturally excluding any pre-existing medical condition – and loss of property (though you may want to check that loss of property isn't already covered by your household insurance). If EU visitors don't get medical insurance, which is strongly recommended, you must at least get the EHIC, which entitles EU members to reciprocal medical care. Drivers must ensure they have at least third-party insurance.

Internet facilities

If you can't download data in Spain as part of your mobile-phone contract, you'll find that many establishments, public and private, offer Wi-Fi. In cities and resorts you'll never be far from a bar which, for the price of a drink, will let you look at your emails. Airports, train and bus stations, hotels, shopping centres and libraries now offer free Wi-Fi access. You may have to ask for the code and put up with slower download speeds than you would like.

L

Language

In cities and coastal resorts English is widely understood and spoken. See page 134 for common Spanish vocabulary.

LGBTQ travellers

Spain was one of the first countries to recognise same-sex marriage. There are plenty of LGBTQ-friendly hotels, clubs and bars in Andalucía, especially on the Costa del Sol. Torremolinos, Málaga and Seville have lively gay scenes. A useful organisation to contact for further information is Colegas (www.

Colourful fans for sale

colegaweb.org). Another useful site is www.gayiberia.com.

M

Media

Print

National Spanish dailies such as *El País*, *El Mundo* and *ABC* have special Andalucían editions printed in Seville. At least one local daily is published in each of Andalucía's provincial capitals. They can be very useful for finding out what events are scheduled in the area and usually include emergency telephone numbers and transport information.

European newspapers are readily available on the Costa del Sol and in larger cities. Some UK dailies print editions in Spain and are distributed in the morning. Otherwise, foreign newspapers are available at midday or early afternoon.

A number of English-language publications serve the large number of expatriates living along the Mediterranean coast. Some of them are free: look for them in supermarkets and touristy bars. They include:

SUR in English (www.surinenglish.com)
Costa del Sol News (www.costa-news.com)
Essential Marbella (www.essentialmagazine.com)
The Olive Press (www.theolivepress.es)

Radio

Radio reception varies considerably across Andalucía depending on prox-imity to urban centres and whether or not there are mountains nearby. Public radio stations include Radio Nacional (RNE1; news and current affairs) and Radio 3 (contemporary music). On the Costa de Sol there are several radio stations that broadcast in English.

Television

There are two nationwide television channels in Spain, TVE 1 and TVE 2, and several private networks including Antena 3, Tele 5 and Canal Plus. Digital services allow for the original language soundtrack of British and US films to be accessed from a menu. Most hotel televisions also get foreign channels by cable or satellite.

Money

Cash machines

Cash machines (ATMs) are located in every high street and can be found all over urban centres. There is at least one in every large town. Look for the sign 'Telebanco'. You can usually select your preferred language. Spanish banks normally don't charge a commission for using ATMs, but your own bank may charge for the currency conversion.

Credit cards

Credit cards are accepted everywhere except very small shops and market stalls – it is wise to have a least a little cash on you for smaller purchases. The most widely used and accepted are Mastercard and Visa.

Newspaper kiosk

Currency

The currency of Spain is the euro, which comes in coins valued 1 euro, 2 euros, plus 50, 20, 10, 5, 2 and 1 cents. Notes (bills) are worth 5, 10, 20, 50, 100, 200 and 500 euros.

Although all prices are marked in euros, some older people occasionally talk in the previous currency, pesetas, or even in 'duros', an informal word for five pesetas.

Taxes

Value-added tax, IVA (*impuesto sobre el valor agregado*), will be added to your hotel and restaurant bills. A higher rate applies to goods and services, including car-hire charges, and lower rate to certain basic necessities. Non-EU citizens can claim back value-added tax (*IVA* in Spanish) on goods and services that cost over €90. To get a refund, you will need to present your passport in the shop and get a receipt which shows the *IVA* component. Show this at the airport or port before you leave.

Tipping

Service is either included in the bill or discretionary, but there are no hard rules. When dining at an averagely smart restaurant, 10 percent of the bill will be appropriate. In other contexts, simply round up the bill to the nearest euro. In an upmarket hotel you may want to tip a porter €1–2 per bag and leave €2–5 for housekeeping if you feel a good job has been done.

Travellers' cheques and changing money

There are money-changing facilities at the airport, but the best rates for cashing travellers' cheques and changing foreign currency are obtained at banks. Outside of normal banking hours, businesses displaying a *cambio* sign will change foreign currency into euros. Larger hotels will also change guests' money, but the exchange rate will be slightly worse than at the bank. Travellers' cheques always get a better rate than cash. Take your passport when changing money or travellers' cheques, for identification purposes.

Post

The Spanish postal service is efficient. Every large town has a post office, generally open Monday–Friday 9am–2pm and 4–7pm and Saturday morning. Most people, however, buy stamps from *estancos*, tobacconist shops that advertise themselves with a 'Tabacos' sign in yellow and brown. Post boxes are painted yellow and may be in two parts – one marked *ciudad* (for local mail) and the other marked *provincias y extranjero* (for the rest of the country and abroad). To send a postcard from Spain to another EU country costs around 60 centimes, 80 centimes for the US.

Semana Santa (Holy Week) in Málaga

R

Religion

The dominant religion of Spain is Roman Catholicism. Around 70 percent of the population professes faith but only an estimated 15 percent attend church regularly. Most cathedrals and churches hold their principal mass on Sunday morning, but there may be services at other times of the week. You are welcome to attend, but if you are just sightseeing discreetly leave and come back when the service is over. Other places of worship, including mosques, should similarly be treated with respect.

S

Smoking

Despite the fact that many people smoke in Spain, the country has very strict laws against smoking in public places. It is officially prohibited in all public indoor spaces, including transport, workplaces and bars and restaurants.

T

Telephones

To call Spain from abroad, tel: +34. Spanish landline numbers all have 9 digits; the area code is an integral part of each number, so you must dial it even for a local call. Numbers beginning 900 are toll-free; 902 numbers are informa-tion lines at rates slightly higher than normal. All mobile numbers begin with a 6 or 7.

Gibraltar, as a British Overseas Territory, is the exception. Its country calling code is +350, which is followed by a standard 8 digits for a landline.

Phone booths (*cabinas*) can still be found at railway stations, but are declining in number and use. Most work with phone cards, which you can buy for various values at *estancos* (tobacco shops), newsstands and other outlets. In cities there are also phone shops (*locutorios*) that can be more convenient and cheaper for making long-distance calls than from a hotel room.

Mobile-phone coverage is good but may be limited in mountainous, under-populated areas. If you are going to spend some time in Spain, it may be worth getting a pay-as-you-go SIM card for your phone – available from specialist shops, hypermarkets or department stores.

To call another country, dial 00 then the country code:
Australia: 61
Ireland: 353
UK: 44
US and Canada: 1

Time zones

Spain is in the CET/CEST (Central European) time zone, which is one hour ahead of Greenwich Mean Time (GMT) in winter and summer. Daylight saving is observed: the clocks go back one hour

Remember to look up: the domed roof of Granada Catedral

on the last Sunday in October and forward on the last Sunday of March.

Toilets

It is rare to find a municipal public toilet in Spain. Invariably your best bet is to have a drink in a bar and use the toilet there. Alternatively, shopping centres and department stores usually have free toilets. There are many expressions for toilet in Spanish: in a public place you are most likely to see *aseos* or *servicios*. In someone's home, you should ask for '*el cuarto de baño*'. The usual signs on toilet doors are *Damas* for women and *Caballeros* for men, though you might also see *Señoras* and *Señores*.

Tourist information

There are tourist-information offices in all the towns of Andalucía offering advice on sightseeing, accommodation and much else. They are generally well signposted, usually situated in or near the main square, making them perfect places to get your bearings.

If you are planning a trip, your first port of call will be the main Spanish tourism website – spain.info – followed by the official website for your chosen region of Andalucía. These sites will direct you to tourist-information websites and offices. The main ones you are likely to need will be:

Seville: Paseo Marqués de Contadero; tel: 955-471 232; http://visita sevilla.es

Costa del Sol: http://visitacostadelsol. com; Malaga Plaza de la Marina; tel: 951-926 020; http://malagaturismo. com

Gibraltar: The Gibraltar Heritage Trust, The Main Guard 13 John Mackintosh Square; tel: +350-2007 4950; www. visitgibraltar.gi

Cordoba: Plaza del Triunfo; tel: 902-201 774; www.turismodecordoba.org; Granada Plaza del Carmen; tel: 958-249 280; http://granadatur.com

Transport

Arrival by air

Andalucía has air links with the rest of Europe and North Africa. There are airports in Almería, Granada, Jerez de la Frontera and Seville, but Málaga is the main airport for the region. Several budget companies operate direct flights from European cities to Andalucía. Transatlantic flights operate into Madrid from where you can switch to a domestic flight.

Arrival by bus

Eurolines (www.eurolines.com) operates bus services from the UK to Andalucía's main cities, including Málaga, Seville, Granada, Algeciras, Almería, Marbella and Córdoba), taking around 30 hours plus depending on changes.

Arrival by car

Spain has an impressive network of motorways. The journey from the French border to Andalucía is all motorway. The

Cycling is a great way to get around Seville

Mediterranean coast route via Barcelona and Valencia can be expensive in tolls; the route through Zaragoza and Madrid is toll-free.

If you are travelling from Britain you might want to consider taking the car ferry from Plymouth to Santander or from Portsmouth to Bilbao (brittany-ferries.co.uk) to shorten the driving time.

Andalucía is also connected to southern Portugal by motorway, via the bridge across the Guadíana River at Ayamonte.

When bringing your own vehicle to Spain you must have third-party insurance (arrange European cover before leaving home), a valid EU or international driving licence, and the vehicle log book/registration document. It is also sensible to get European breakdown cover.

Arrival by sea

Several companies operate regular vehicle and passenger ferries between Almería, Motril, Málaga, Algeciras, Tarifa and Cádiz, and ports on the African coast and on the Canary Islands. The main ones are Trasmediterranea (www.trasmediterranea.es), Baleària (www.balearia.com), FRS (www.frs.es) and Naviera Armas (www.navieraarmas.com).

Arrival by train

Rail travel to Spain from other European countries can be organised through Rail Europe (raileurope.com), which offers a variety of saver passes for different periods of travel. A high-speed AVE line links Madrid with Seville and Madrid with Malaga.

Getting around by bus

Buses reach more places than trains and can be cheaper. To find out about routes, times and fares go to the local *Estacion de Autobuses* (bus station) or ask at the tourist-information office.

The main company serving inter-city routes in Andalucía is Alsina Graells (tel: 902-422 242; www.alsa.es).

Getting around by bicycle

Cycling is a good way to enjoy the beauty of Andalucía's scenery, though intense heat makes it hard going in summer. A good map is required if you want to get off the main roads, but even then you may find that you have to ask the locals if you want to take the quietest backroads. The region has several *vías verdes* (www.viasverdes.com) – cycling and hiking routes running along disused railway lines. Bicycles can be hired in most resorts on a daily or weekly basis.

Getting around by car
Hiring a car

To hire a car you need to be over 21 and possess a valid EU or international driving licence. US and Canadian licences are also usually accepted, but you should check the exact requirements with the car hire company when you make the booking. It is cheaper to arrange car hire before you arrive. Be

Wandering around Granada

aware that car hire companies may ask you for a provisional credit card payment as a deposit: if you return the car intact the sum will not be debited from your account.

Rules of the road

Drive on the right, overtake on the left. Give way to traffic coming from the right. Speed limits are 50kph (30mph) in built-up areas, 90–100kph (55–60mph) on highways and 120kph (75mph) on motorways. A reflective yellow jacket for roadside emergencies must be carried in the passenger compartment of the vehicle. The use of seat belts (front and back seats) is obligatory. A red warning triangle must be carried. Motorcycle riders and their passengers must wear crash helmets. Spanish roads are patrolled by the motorcycle police of the *Guardia Civil*. They can impose on-the-spot fines for common offences including speeding, travelling too close to the car in front and driving with burned-out lights.

Getting around by train

Andalucía has an efficient rail network that is good for particular journeys, such as Seville to Jerez de la Frontera, but it doesn't reach everywhere. For information and tickets see www.renfe.com/EN/viajeros/.

Getting around on foot

There are many well-marked hiking trails in the countryside. If you want to go for a hike, however short or long, go well prepared with suitable clothing, suncream and enough water – and always let someone know where you are going and when you expect to get back.

Visas and passports

EU citizens can enter Spain with a valid ID card or passport. Citizens from countries such as the USA, Canada, Australia and New Zealand don't need a visa either for a stay of up to 90 days (renewable). Citizens of other countries should check with the Ministry of Internal Affairs website (www.interior.gob.es) to see if they require a visa.

Weights and measures

Spain uses the metric system: grams and kilograms for weights in shops and airport luggage scales; metres and kilometres for distances; metres for the heights of mountains and mountain passes; and litres for liquid measures. Some traditional Spanish weights and measures are still in use. These include: *fanega* (6,460 sq metres); *arroba* (11.5kg); and *quintal* (4 *arrobas*).

Women travellers

Women have equal rights to men in Spain and female travellers, whether alone or accompanied, should have no particular problems as long as they take the normal, sensible precautions.

LANGUAGE

The language of Andalucía is Spanish, sometimes known as Castilian. It is a Romance language, derived from Latin, enriched by words from Arabic left by the Islamic civilisation of Spain.

Spanish is a phonetic language: words are pronounced exactly as they are spelt. It uses two verbs to mean 'to be' and has two ways for one person to address another, formal and informal.

Andalucía has a strong regional accent that may take some getting used to if you have learned your Spanish elsewhere. In particular, they do not pronounce the last 's' of words, so 'dos euros' (two euros) sounds like 'do euro'.

English is widely spoken in the cities and wherever tourists go, notably the Costa del Sol where there are also many English-speaking residents. English is the official language of Gibraltar.

Useful words and phrases

Hello *Hola*
How are you? *¿Cómo está usted?*
How much is it? *¿Cuánto es?*
What is your name? *¿Cómo se llama usted?*
My name is… *Yo me llamo…*
I don't understand *No entiendo*
Please speak more slowly *Hable más despacio, por favor*

Can you help me? *¿Me puede ayudar?*
I'm sorry *Lo siento*
I don't know *No lo se*
No problem *No hay problema*
Let's go *Vámonos*
See you tomorrow *Hasta mañana*
See you soon *Hasta pronto*
At what time? *¿A qué hora?*
When? *¿Cuándo?*
What time is it? *¿Qué hora es?*
yes *sí*
no *no*
please *por favor*
thank you (very much) *(muchas) gracias*
you're welcome *de nada*
excuse me *perdóneme*
goodbye *adiós*
good evening/night *buenas tardes/ noches*
today *hoy*
yesterday *ayer*
tomorrow *mañana* (note: *mañana* also means 'morning')
now *ahora*
later *después*
right away *ahora mismo*
this morning *esta mañana*
this afternoon *esta tarde*
this evening *esta tarde*
tonight *esta noche*

Directions

I am looking for… *Estoy buscando…*
Where is…? *¿Dónde está…?*

Ceramic letters

here *aquí*
over there *allí*
the road to… *la carretera a…*
left *izquierda*
right *derecha*
straight on *todo recto*
far *lejos*
near *cerca*
opposite *frente a*
beside *al lado de*
at the end *al final*

Travelling

I want to get off at… *Quiero bajarme en…*
Is there a bus to the museum *¿Hay un autobús al museo?*
What street is this? *¿Qué calle es ésta?*
Which line do I take for…? *¿Qué línea cojo para?*
How far is…? *¿A qué distancia está…?*
airport *aeropuerto*
customs *aduana*
railway station *estación de tren*
bus station *estación de autobuses*
metro station *estación de metro*
bus *autobús*
bus stop *parada de autobús*
platform *apeadero*
ticket *billete*
return ticket *billete de ida y vuelta*
hitch-hiking *auto-stop*
toilets *servicios*

Eating out

breakfast *desayuno*
lunch *almuerzo/comida*

dinner *cena*
meal *comida*
made to order *por encargo*
drink included *incluida bebida/con-sumición*
wine list *carta de vinos*
the bill *la cuenta*
waiter, please! *camarero, por favour*
knife *cuchillo*
fork *tenedor*
spoon *cuchara*
plate *plato*
glass *vaso*
napkin *servietta*
ashtray *cenicero*

Days of the week

Monday *lunes*
Tuesday *martes*
Wednesday *miércoles*
Thursday *jueves*
Friday *viernes*
Saturday *sábado*
Sunday *domingo*

Months of the year

January *enero*
February *febrero*
March *marzo*
April *abril*
May *mayo*
June *junio*
July *julio*
August *agosto*
September *septiembre*
October *octubre*
November *noviembre*
December *diciembre*

On the set of Lawrence of Arabia

BOOKS AND FILM

Andalucía has a long history of inspiring itinerant authors and artists. An anthology of the region can read like a who's who of distinguished travellers. The books that they subsequently published give a good insight into the place, past and present. They were usually struck by the colours, the bright Mediterranean light, the excitement of events and the exuberant life of the people; although some of them left not eulogising but cursing the place for a variety of reasons from 'everything was soaked in olive oil' to 'unfortunately we didn't meet any bandits in the sierras'.

In the 20th century, Andalucía was rediscovered as a film set: here were superb locations that could either stand in as lookalikes for other places or form beautiful backdrops in their own right. The desert of Almería famously came to be used as a cut-priced Wild West, but a lot of other landscapes and monuments have been used too.

Authors and filmmakers continue to flock here year on year. Here's a selection of those that are most worth tracking down.

Books

A Rose for Winter by Laurie Lee. The author returns to Andalucía in the 1950s.
A Handbook for Travellers in Spain by Richard Ford. Classic 19th-century travel book about Spain.

Sunny Side Up by David Baird. Old and new values collide in a traditional Andalucían village.
South From Granada by Gerald Brenan. An account of the author's experiences living in an Andalucían village in the 1920s.
Tales of the Alhambra by Washington Irving. The 19th-century American author's account of Moorish legends is still enjoyable.
The Road from Ronda by Alastair Boyd. Vivid account of a horse-ride through the Serranía de Ronda.
Death in the Afternoon by Ernest Hemingway. Hemingway's colourful explanation of the bullfight, although much maligned by purists, is still informative and gripping.
Federico García Lorca: A Life by Ian Gibson. Fascinating biography of the Granada-born writer.
Or I'll Dress You in Mourning by Larry Collins and Dominique Lapierre. Brilliant insights into Spain's post-Civil War hardships that moulded the Andalucían matador El Cordobés.
Driving Over Lemons by Chris Stewart. Amusing autobiographical account of an Englishman living the good life in the Alpujarras.
Duende: A Journey in Search of Flamenco by Jason Webster. An Anglo-American's foray into the world of flamenco.

The Return by Victoria Hislop. Romantic but harrowing novel about love and loss in Granada during the Spanish Civil War.

The Factory of Light by Michael Jacobs. A British writer's account of the reality of life in an Andalucían village in the 21st century.

The Moor's Last Stand by Elizabeth Drayson. The story of Boabdil, the last Muslim king of Granada.

The Flavours of Andalucía by Elisabeth Luard. A good introduction to the region's cuisine with recipes from each of the provinces.

Spanish Wine Guide by David and Jennifer Raezer. An insightful overview of the region's wines and sherries.

Costa del Sol by Des Wilson. Thriller about shady shenanigans on the Costa del Crime.

Film and TV series

Game of Thrones (2011–present). The cult fantasy series has used Andalucían locations as backdrops for several episodes, notably the Real Alcázar in Seville, which appears in season 5.

Die Another Day (2002). Pierce Brosnan, as James Bond, is supposedly having adventures in Havana, but for convenience the port city of Cádiz was used as a stand-in for the Cuban capital.

Star Wars Episode II: Attack of the Clones (2002). When Anakin and Padme walk in the Palace grounds they are actually in the Plaza de España in Seville.

The Good, the Bad and the Ugly (1966). In the 1960s, the desert around Tabernas in central Almería was used as a lookalike for the Wild West by European filmmakers on a budget, notably the Italian director Sergio Leone.

Indiana Jones and the Last Crusade (1989). Monsul beach on the Cabo de Gata is used for the scene in Steven Spielberg's film in which Indiana and his father are attacked by a fighter plane and save themselves by scaring up a flock of seagulls.

Lawrence of Arabia (1962). David Lean's epic in the Arabian desert made extensive use of Andalucía: the coast of Almería and various buildings in Seville.

2001: A Space Odyssey (1968). The lunar landscapes in Stanley Kubrick's sci-fi classic were shot in the Tabernas desert of Almería.

The Smurfs (2011). To celebrate the launch of this children's film, the whole of Júzcar (Málaga), previously a white town, was painted a vivid shade of blue. The villagers have a reputation for mushroom harvesting; the smurfs, of course, live in mushroom-shaped dwellings.

Eldorado (1992–93). The BBC's attempt to make a soap opera in the sun, about a group of British expats, only lasted a year before being axed. The fictional town of Los Barcos is really Coín in the province of Málaga.

ABOUT THIS BOOK

This Explore Guide has been produced by the editors of Insight Guides, whose books have set the standard for visual travel guides since 1970. With top-quality photography and authoritative recommendations, these guidebooks bring you the very best routes and itineraries in the world's most exciting destinations.

BEST ROUTES

The routes in the book provide something to suit all budgets, tastes and trip lengths. As well as covering the destination's many classic attractions, the itineraries track lesser-known sights. The routes embrace a range of interests, so whether you are an art fan, a gourmet, a history buff or have kids to entertain, you will find an option to suit.

We recommend reading the whole of a route before setting out. This should help you to familiarise yourself with it and enable you to plan where to stop for refreshments – options are shown in the 'Food and Drink' box at the end of each tour.

For our pick of the tours by theme, consult Recommended Routes for… (see pages 6–7).

INTRODUCTION

The routes are set in context by this introductory section, giving an overview of the destination to set the scene, plus background information on food and drink, shopping and more, while a succinct history timeline highlights the key events over the centuries.

DIRECTORY

Also supporting the routes is a Directory chapter, with a clearly organised A–Z of practical information, our pick of where to stay while you are there and select restaurant listings; these eateries complement the more low-key cafés and restaurants that feature within the routes and are intended to offer a wider choice for evening dining. Also included here are some nightlife listings, plus a handy language guide and our recommendations for books and films about the destination.

ABOUT THE AUTHOR

Nick Inman, a journalist, travel writer and photographer, has a long association with Insight Guides. He has written, edited or contributed to more than 60 books on Spain and France. Nick has been exploring the sights and backroads of Andalucía for the last 25 years.

CONTACT THE EDITORS

We hope you find this Explore Guide useful, interesting and a pleasure to read. If you have any questions or feedback on the text, pictures or maps, please do let us know. If you have noticed any errors or outdated facts, or have suggestions for places to include on the routes, we would be delighted to hear from you. Please drop us an email at hello@insightguides.com. Thanks!

CREDITS

Explore Andalucía
Editor: Helen Fanthorpe
Author: Nick Inman
Head of DTP and Pre-press: Rebeka Davies
Update Production: Apa Digital
Picture Editor: Aude Vauconsant
Cartography: Carte
Photo credits: Alamy 34, 78, 82, 109L, 112, 113, 114, 115, 117, 118, 119; Corrie Wingate/Apa Publications 4MC, 4MC, 4MR, 4ML, 6TL, 7MR, 8ML, 8MC, 12/13, 20, 28MC, 28MR, 32, 33, 35, 47, 48/49, 65, 87L, 86/87, 88, 92, 92/93; Damien Simonis/Rough Guides 4MR; Demetrio Carrasco/Rough Guides 38; Georgie Scott/ Rough Guides 28ML, 49L; Getty Images 73, 104MR, 107, 108/109, 110, 111, 116, 121, 136, 137; iStock 1, 4ML, 6BC, 7T, 7MR, 7M, 8MR, 8MR, 8/9T, 10, 11, 12, 13L, 14/15, 16, 16/17, 18, 21, 24, 24/25, 26, 27, 28MR, 28ML, 29T, 31L, 30/31, 36/37, 42/43, 46, 48, 50, 51, 53, 54/55, 57L, 56/57, 58, 59, 61, 63, 66/67, 70, 71T, 72, 74, 75L, 76, 77, 79L, 84, 85, 89, 90/91, 93L, 96, 97, 98, 99L, 98/99, 101, 102/103, 104ML, 104MC, 104MC, 104ML, 104/105T, 106, 108, 122, 123, 127, 128, 130, 131, 132, 133, 134; Museo Picasso Malaga 8MC; Jorge Zapata/Epa/REX/Shut- terstock 120; Kevin Jones/APA Publications 62; Shutterstock 4/5T, 6MC, 6ML, 8ML, 17L, 19, 22/23, 28MC, 30, 39, 40, 41L, 40/41, 44/45, 52, 56, 60, 64, 68/69, 71MC, 70/71T, 74/75, 78/79, 80/81, 83, 86, 94, 95, 100, 104MR, 124, 125, 126, 129, 135
Cover credits: iStock (main&bottom)

Printed by CTPS – China

First Edition 2018

DISTRIBUTION

UK, Ireland and Europe
Apa Publications (UK) Ltd
sales@insightguides.com
United States and Canada
Ingram Publisher Services
ips@ingramcontent.com
Australia and New Zealand
Woodslane
info@woodslane.com.au
Southeast Asia
Apa Publications (Singapore) Pte
singaporeoffice@insightguides.com
Worldwide
Apa Publications (UK) Ltd
sales@insightguides.com

SPECIAL SALES, CONTENT LICENSING AND COPUBLISHING

Insight Guides can be purchased in bulk quantities at discounted prices. We can create special editions, personalised jackets and corporate imprints tailored to your needs.
sales@insightguides.com
www.insightguides.biz

INDEX

MAP LEGEND

- ● Start of tour
- — Tour & route direction
- ❶ Recommended sight
- ❷ Recommended restaurant/café
- ★ Place of interest
- ❶ Tourist information
- ✈ Airport
- ⎯⎯⋅ Ferry route
- Ⓜ Metro station
- 🇮 Statue/monument
- ✚ † Church
- † Monastery
- ✉ Main post office
- 🚌 Main bus station
- ⊕ Hospital
- ✳ Viewpoint
- ⁙ Ancient site
- 🏰 Castle
- ⚑ Beach
- 🕳 Cave
-     Park
-     Important building
-     Transport hub
-     Urban area
-     National park

INSIGHT ⊙ GUIDES

OFF THE SHELF

Since 1970, INSIGHT GUIDES has provided a unique perspective on the world's best travel destinations by using specially commissioned photography and illuminating text written by local authors.

Whether you're planning a city break, a walking tour or the journey of a lifetime, our superb range of guidebooks and phrasebooks will inspire you to discover more about your chosen destination.

INSIGHT GUIDES

offer a unique combination of stunning photos, absorbing narrative and detailed maps, providing all the inspiration and information you need.

PHRASEBOOKS & DICTIONARIES

help users to feel at home, when away. Pocket-sized with a free app to download, they go where you do.

CITY GUIDES

pack hundreds of great photos into a smaller format with detailed practical information, so you can navigate the world's top cities with confidence.

EXPLORE GUIDES

feature easy-to-follow walks and itineraries in the world's most exciting destinations, with our choice of the best places to eat and drink along the way.

POCKET GUIDES

combine concise information on where to go and what to do in a handy compact format, ideal on the ground. Includes a full-colour, fold-out map.

EXPERIENCE GUIDES

feature offbeat perspectives and secret gems for experienced travellers, with a collection of over 100 ideas for a memorable stay in a city.

www.insightguides.com